DANGER ZONE

Christian Leadership in Crisis...What Next?

Bernie Lutchman

DANGER ZONE
Copyright © 2011 by Bernie Lutchman
Cover Design by Greg Borawski
Published by: Theocentric Publishing Group
1069 Main St.
Chipley, Florida 32428

http://www.theocentricpublishing.com

All rights reserved. No part of this book may be reproduced or transmitted in any form or by any means without written permission of the author.

Unless otherwise noted, all Scripture are from the New King James Version (NKJV) of the Bible. Copyright © 1982 by Thomas Nelson, Inc.

New Living Translation (NLT) Holy Bible. New Living Translation copyright © 1996, 2004 by Tyndale Charitable Trust. Used by permission of Tyndale House Publishers.

New International Version Copyright, NIV, 1973, 1978, 1984, International Bible Society.

Amplified Bible (AMP) Copyright © 1954, 1958, 1962, 1964, 1965, 1987 by The Lockman Foundation

New American Standard Bible (NASB) Copyright © 1960, 1962, 1963, 1968, 1971, 1972, 1973, 1975, 1977, 1995 by The Lockman Foundation

Library of Congress Control Number 2011929286

ISBN 9780983244110

DEDICATION

Christ is the main Source but He uses many people who are responsible for my peace, joy and contentment.

First and foremost is my dear wife Vicki Lutchman, who has inspired and fired me up to be the man of God I aspired to be.

Secondly, my children – Bernie, Sam and Sarah – who put up with me sitting behind this computer.

To my dear brother Bruce Assaf, who wrote the foreword of this book, thank you! Bruce is the head of Blow the Trumpet International Ministries, Atlanta, Ga.

To Dr. James Merritt, former president of the Southern Baptist Convention (2000-2002), whose farewell presidential sermon in St Louis, Missouri in 2002 refocused my life to think on these things, thank you.

To Dr. Joe White, the powerful leader of Men at the Cross, whose message of the Cross changed my life forever on September 7, 2001, four days before 911 and is a good friend.

Foreword

Bruce Assaf, Director
Blow The Trumpet International Ministries

In many years of ministry I have encountered countless brothers and sisters in Christ with true servant hearts for Jesus. They stand out as a result of their humility and the fruit they produce making them powerful witness for Christ. When Jesus looked at Nathaniel and said "Here is a true Israelite indeed there is no guile." When I read that scripture my thoughts and heart go to Bernie Lutchman. While none of us have in no way arrived, all press toward the mark; Bernie presses toward the mark for that prize, Jesus Christ, with a focused faith and relentless service. On my first encounter with Bernie I knew here was a brother in Christ whom was not only serving Jesus from a sincere heart, but was a genuine bondservant of the Lord, serving God's people in a selfless way.

I have found Bernie Lutchman to be that man of God that has consistently displayed a Christ like character whom encourages and touches lives around him in a wonderful way. Bernie's walk with the Lord has revealed to me the true meaning of working integrity in all those he comes in contact with. I have been one of the many that has been so greatly encouraged and blessed through someone like Bernie who truly desires to exhort and esteem others better than themselves, in furthering the cause of Christ in their own lives and ministry. A true servant that aptly qualified him to write this new book

Bernie's life and ministry transcends beyond denominational walls and barriers, yet the Lord has given Bernie the needed understanding of God's extensive family, and like a modern day Paul, reflecting and putting into practice the unique gift of being "all things to all people" without compromise of the Gospel and it's message.

Bernie's ministry is an extension of who Bernie Lutchman is. He is first and foremost focused on the Cross of Christ, and with that saving knowledge his obedience has allowed him to impart nuggets of truth in speaking the wisdom of God through God's Word imparting those needed insights into the Body of Christ.

As with his last book, "Two Minute Warning" Bernie continues in bringing to his reader a broad overview of God's Word with a timely and needed message in a venue without losing focus on key spiritual points. He has brought clarity to those issues that pertain to the believers need of hearing and applying to their lives. He desires for theme to experience the victory that is theirs in Christ. Bernie's heart clearly reveals the burden, care, compassion and concern he has for the Church and the anointing God has given him in touching the lives of both sheep and shepherd alike.

As you open your heart to the message of "Danger Zone" and carefully consider and mediate on each page read, you will be wonderfully blessed, inspired, encouraged, but most of all challenged. Challenged to face and appropriate what Bernie has brought to light in this exciting book for those truly seeking a closer and more intimate walk with their Lord.

It is evident that Bernie aims to hit the mark with this book in all it relates to, having God's Word and its application directed and targeted into your heart and life. Bernie covers every area, every corner, hitting the mark in bringing the truth of God's Word to his reader and in all humility and honesty. It's a bull's eye!

Bruce W. Assaf
Author/Speaker/Missionary
Blow The Trumpet International Ministries
www.blowthetrumpetintl.com

Table of Contents

1 Critical Biblical Leadership for the 21st Century 1
2 Persistent Perseverance 13
3 Leaving a Living Legacy 37
4 Leadership 1.0 59
5 Leadership 2.0 79
6 Fourth and Goal 99
7 Christ in the Zone 121

1 Critical Biblical Leadership for the 21st Century

> *Right into the Danger Zone*
> *You'll never say hello to you*
> *Until you get it on the red line overload*
> *You'll never know what you can do*
> *Until you get it up as high as you can go*
> *Out along the edges*
> *Always where I burn to be*
> *The further on the edge*
> *The hotter the intensity*
> *Highway to the Danger Zone*
>
> Kenny Loggins, written by Giorgio Moroder and Tom Whitlock, 1986

These are dangerous times, not just for everyone, but for men especially fathers, sons, young boys; just about any man who not only enters the door of a church but who lives on this earth.

The average Western male faces a difficult time meeting expectations, ingrained from birth. The post depression boom created a middle class where success had came to be defined as not just a good job with the house in the suburbs, chicken in every pot and a '49 Ford in the driveway, but a college education, wife and 2 ½ kids! Over the past decades, things changed. The formula is not so sure to succeed anymore.

The major problem with man-made formulae is they are man-made! The Lord has ordained America and the Western world and blessed us with so many incredible things, that the post- World War II prosperity culture seemingly worked for a long time.

The 1950's were a time of great wealth. The creation of the Interstate highway system and the jobs to go with it expanded the US beyond belief. The term "suburban sprawl" became well known at this time. America was on the move into the rest of this great country. But the seeds of secularism were already being sown. The "Greatest Generation" won World War II, but they began the slide which lost our children today.

As riches abounded, comfort and easy believism abounded even more. Some well known protestant denominations began removing mention of the Blood of Christ from their sermons – the Same Blood which cleansed you and me from our sins. Churches became more social meeting places with sterilized worship services. Sure Billy Graham and others were having great success at massive evangelistic crusades all over the country. But serious preachers such as J. Vernon McGee, A.W. Tozer and others were warning us over 50 years ago of things we would see today. No one listened.

It would not serve any purpose to list the churches, denominations or conferences which started the church's slide into apostasy and eventually final death on judgment day. What is needed in these critical times, where not only the days are short but events are rapidly heading for a showdown with biblical destiny, is acknowledgement of the problem – repentance – and restoration…..all in this specific order.

This is what the book you are holding, DANGER ZONE, seeks to do for the man or woman of God. We seek, through the Word of God, not just to provide the way to repentance and true restoration to Christ and biblical leadership, but to take note of the warning signs that are everywhere in these last days.

You may not think this applies to any of us, but read again from Jeremiah 2:13 (NLT).

"For my people have done two evil things:
    They have abandoned me—the fountain of living water.
    And they have dug for themselves cracked cisterns that can hold no water at all!

DANGER ZONE

This book is not about banging folks over the head all the way through. This chapter explains the premise and the foundation of our Spirit led discussion and the pro-active solutions we need to apply. We take instructions from this verse and return to the Fountain of Living Water. We abandon the broken and cracked cisterns that spill water faster than we can pour it on. This is so, because we were not designed to be conned by the sellers of worldly water carriers, but were created to drink of and bathe in the Fountain of Living Water.

The prophet Jeremiah speaks not just to the lost people of Judah around 586 BC, but the wandering sheep of Jesus, now floundering as the end of all things come to a close.

THEMES

Legacy, Leadership and Living effectively in the Fourth Quarter of Life are the only three themes of this book. However, these three rest on Three Pillars – Christ, the Holy Spirit and perseverance. The Foundation is God, the Father.

Why is perseverance a Pillar? Scripture says so! Romans 5:3-4 "And not only that, but we also glory in tribulations, knowing that tribulation produces perseverance; and perseverance, character; and character, hope."

Godly perseverance is based on Christ, who is our Hope. We stand on this Hope as a significant Pillar of our faith in God. Along with Christ and the Holy Spirit, we are now built into the fabric of Heaven, from the foundations of the earth.

Just as trusting Christ, as Lord and Savior is the step to eternal life, if those making a profession of faith do not persevere or worse even walk away from the faith, a fiery end awaits them. This is why the verse the Apostle Paul had what are the second Famous Last Words in the Bible (the first being – IT IS FINISHED).

In 2 Timothy 4:7 Paul gave some of his final words before being executed by the decadent evil Roman Emperor Nero; "I have fought the good fight, I have finished the race, I have kept the faith."

The most radically saved man in the Bible, who had seen the living Messiah minister in Jerusalem for three years and then killed his followers, persevered.

- One does not fight the good fight without staying in the battle.
- One does not finish the race, without staying the course.
- One does not remain filled with Faith, without staying in Christ.
- Abide with Him. Abide in Him. Abide alongside Him.

LEGACY

My research led me to a descendant of the family tree of Abraham Lincoln! Lincoln himself has no living offspring here in Central Illinois. However, his family tree extends all the way past the great preacher Jonathan Edwards to the Puritan Obadiah Holmes. Holmes is significant in American Christian history because it was he and Roger Williams who escaped to what is now Providence, and started the Baptist church in America in the brand new state of Rhode Island!

All of this information about Lincoln's tree came from a descendant of Edward Wightman, the last man burnt at the stake by the King of England. Ron Wightman blessed me with this information about his famous ancestor who is listed in Foxe's Book of Martyrs!

Each one of us wants to leave a legacy. For what other reason would we decide to marry, have children and plan the best life possible for them? Why work so hard to get all this "stuff"? The answers are obvious. Godly parents leave godly legacies. There is no doubt about it. Sure, sometimes an offspring or two slips through the cracks, but each man is responsible for his own choices.

Francis Schaefer (1912-1984) is known as the father of modern American Evangelicalism. His work was foremost in apologetics and set out the standard for what we know operate in as "evangelicals". He set the standard for writing on the biblical worldview of culture, citizenship and the church. He even foresaw the current evangelical crack-up in "The Great Evangelical Disaster". Yet his own son, Frank, has denied the faith and magnificent work of his father and turned to the world systems. He is now celebrated by the secular media as an 'enlightened Christian". Whenever the world loves a so-called "Christian author, leader or pastor", run as far from him or her as you can!

Genesis 49 is one of the greatest records of Legacy in History. I encourage you to read this thorough, yet brief, history of all the twelve sons of Jacob (Israel). As he was about to die, the Bible records each blessing on each son. I traced the end or the fruit of these final blessings and the results are astonishing. How each tribe ended up some good, most bad, is a dire warning for God's people especially.

LEADERSHIP

My examination of the leadership style of God's great General Joshua revealed the richness of the Word of God and what His standard really is for biblical leadership.

The character attributes of Joshua are not much different from any faithful servant of God. The only difference is who he was. The man was not just Moses' understudy but the chosen instrument to lead the Israelites into the Promised Land of Canaan. Even his name is significant. The name Joshua in the original Hebrew language, translates into Yehoshua or in short Yeshua – Jesus! Joshua led captives into the Promised Land; King Jesus leads us (captives to sin) into the Promised Kingdom!

There is one pitfall in modern leadership and this can be found a lot in ministry. It is found in the regular church or the parachurch organizations and believe it or not the home. It is called burnout. The prime biblical example of this is Moses. What an amazing story this is! After studying the Word of God in Exodus and several ancient Jewish rabbinical writings, it was revealed how this small (and sometimes treated as insignificant) story of Moses and Jethro changed the course of the history of our faith!

How so? Well, here is the Word of God from Exodus chapter 18. I suggest the entire chapter be read again. Verses 17-20 (NLT) are important for understanding the purpose of this discussion.

"This is not good!" Moses' father-in-law exclaimed. You are going to wear yourself out and the people, too. This job is too heavy a burden for you to handle all by yourself. Now listen to me, and let me give you a word of advice, and may God be with you. You should continue to be the people's representative before God, bringing their disputes to him. Teach them God's decrees, and give them his instructions. Show them how to conduct their lives."

In God's marketplace, we are all CEO's (Chief Executive Officers). This is the main difference between the world's business managers and those who manage God's business at home or in Kingdom work.

Jethro, Moses' father in law, is a study in itself that could take up volumes. He had many names from Reuel (Hebrew for a friend of God) to Yitro (or Jethro that actually is a title, meaning His Excellency being a Midianite priest of a pagan religion). This is important because the ancient sages and rabbis, who came out of the desert with Joshua and their scribes, had many stories about Jethro. He was said to be a direct descendant of Abraham yet was a high priest of an unknown religion. This is gleaned from the Scriptures.

So here was a NOT a man of God, upon HEARING the accounts of the real God – Yahweh – instantly becoming a believer in the God of Moses and his own father Abraham! This confirms the New Testament of "faith comes by hearing, and hearing by the Word of God."

He observes Moses daily routine of long lines of probably, distraught Israelites lined up for hours upon hours, waiting to have their disputes resolved. Horrified at what he saw, Jethro calls Moses on the carpet. He had noticed the elders of Israel standing around doing nothing, while Moses did all the work. By then, Jethro was a saved man, sent by God, to set up the judicial system we still use in the 21st Century!

God through Jethro says, taken from Exodus 18:17-20:

- This is not good. (INSIGHT)
- You are going to wear yourself out. (INTUITION)
- The job is too big for you to handle alone. (INSTRUCTION)
- You will listen to Me (God). (INSTANT OBEDIENCE)
- You will continue to represent the people before God. (INTERCESSION)
- You will bring their disputes to Him. (INTERVENTION)
- You will teach them His decrees or commands. (IMPARTATION)
- You will impart to them, His basic instructions before leaving earth (b.i.b.l.e). (ILLUSTRATION)
- You will model for them HOW to live their lives. (IMITATION OF CHRIST...see Hebrews 11:23-26)

How did Jethro set up the modern judicial system of "chief justice" all the way down to the smallest judge and administrator? Scholars have agreed with this for many thousands of years. Here is how God set it up. God used Jethro for this instruction. "But select from all the people some capable, honest men who fear God and hate bribes. Appoint them as leaders over groups of one thousand, one hundred, fifty, and ten. They should always be available to solve the people's common disputes, but have them bring the major cases to you. Let the leaders decide the smaller matters themselves. They will help you carry the load, making the task easier for you" (Exodus 18: 21-22, NLT).

The last time God said "this is not good" about another man, was when He created woman. The LORD said it was not good that man was alone. Therefore, He made man a helper – Eve. This is what God meant our wives to be. More than a helper, the actual Hebrew words "Ezer Kenegho" carries power, strength and the sense of completing the man in a relationship.

As leaders in the home first and then the rest of God's Kingdom, we are assigned certain stations in life. The home is where biblical leadership must begin – as a father or increasingly, in the 21st century, as a single parent. While God's ideal is for a man and woman to be married and raising children, no one should ever diminish the great women and men who are raising young ones alone, in the midst of difficult circumstances or for that matter, those who choose to remain single! Remember, the Apostle Paul, the leader of the New Testament Church and apostle to the Gentiles, was himself a single man.

The two chapters in this book on leadership go into some depth on how this Biblical leadership can be put into practice on the most basic level. However, for all of this biblical knowledge to work, there MUST be a spirit of obedience.

Jethro was a man under Kingdom Authority. Therefore, he had the right to tell his son-in-law Moses "you will listen" to me and do the following: Intercede in prayer on behalf of your people; bring their prayer requests to God and then teach them EVERYTHING God said in His Word! This is NOT the just the work of the pastor of a church. This is the obligation of each man and woman of God, whether you are in men's, or women's or children's ministry. Live a life full of the imitation of Christ, while imparting His Word to the next generation. This is our calling.

LIVING

Jethro told Moses, in verse 20 – "you will show them how to conduct their lives"! SHOW equals walk the talk. Moses did lose his temper and because of striking the Rock, he was not allowed to enter the Promised Land, but would die in the desert. This account is in Numbers 20: 1-13.

His conduct here was open disobedience to God who told him to SPEAK to the Rock (which 1 Corinthians 10:4 said was Christ)!

Therefore, the Third theme listed in this book is Living, living well and living effectively and obediently. Basically, living with the Fourth Quarter of Life in mind! Many will think "we have time, we're young. What's this fourth quarter stuff? Isn't that for a bunch of middle-aged guys coming to the end of their lives?" "I am young and have many years to go"!

Oh yeah? No one knows how long God has given us to live, with fleeting breath, on this earth. Oswald Chambers the author of My Utmost For His Highest died at age 43. The great American missionary Jim Elliott (husband of the well-known author Elizabeth) was killed in January 1956 at age 28 by people he went to help. The movie "End of the Spear" is about his life. These are well known examples…there are more, of regular people like you and I, who never make it to 50 years of age. Would they have lived life any differently, discipled more, done more for the Kingdom of Heaven? Would they? But why didn't they?

Many young Christians may have great intentions of doing more with their lives in the service of the Lord, but are suddenly called home or are side-tracked by career, work, family obligations or the pursuit of leisure. More and more we see more stressed out young couples, young professionals and even middle-aged ones. When harsh economic times hit and even Christian folks are stressed out, somehow the Work of Christ ends up taking the entire back seat and the trunk.

However, the life lived in the power of Christ is well anointed and full of total inner peace, even when circumstances move us into the Danger Zone. It is almost impossible to avoid stressful situations on the job – where more is expected for less – or at home, where the cost of living keeps climbing with demands from family members in different stages of life.

The issue of obedience also ties in to living with the Fourth Quarter in mind. Each day of a life lived in the Spirit, walked with obedience and submission to the Father, brings us one day closer to being sanctified and more and more worthy of His calling.

LIVING WITH STRESS

While not a medical professional, the Lord has given me insight into certain topics to share with fellow believers, in order to exhibit the sufficiency of Scripture. To wit, there are two types of stress – good and bad!

The good stress is temporary and short-lived. You have seen it, for example, in a football game with 2 minutes to go and one team has 80 yards to go to score a touchdown to win the game. The great Denver Broncos QB John Elway excelled in the two-minute drill and more often than not, answered these moments of testing the mettle of a man, with flourish (and usually a Bronco victory). The stress of facing a goal line stand from a combined 1200 lbs opposing force field, on the line, with 15 seconds left, is enough for fans to bite their nails off!

The bad stress leads to death, stroke and other less dire side effects. We have all gone through this – the shooting pains in the eyes, the stomach acid and the pains at the back of the neck.

What stress does is attack the body's Nervous System. I am talking the entire system of neurons, neurochemicals and all their allied structures. The nervous system controls every aspect of bodily activity and motion. These include the brain, nerves, ganglia and spinal cord. The ganglia are similar to an internet server. It is a cluster of nerve cells and the crucial to the entire nervous system.

Any of us, who are alive and part of the American work force, face the same challenges. Each of us has the same type of body structure, having been created by the same God. Therefore, we are all susceptible to the same chemical reactions of the body, only in varying degrees.

Christ spoke about stress in Matthew 6:34 "So do not worry about tomorrow; for tomorrow will care for itself. Each day has enough trouble of its own." You and I know what worry and stress can lead to.

A stressed out Christian, or anyone else, in today's world of falling/failing expectations can feel ambushed. The sense of being attacked this way, leads to anger. The reaction to this anger can lead to multiple responses – alcohol, adultery, pornography, apathy and a host of other un-Christ-like things.

This anger can lead to the man or woman of God feeling totally alone. However, we are NOT alone! We can refuse to participate with the world as it wallows in a whirlwind of worry.

We have the Power of Christ in us. The final chapter of this book gives a brief summary of some of America's most famous men, their faith or lack of and how they viewed life. There over dozens of biblical names for the Source of Life – Christ and the corresponding verses to go with each. It is imperative to pray each verse, and I show you how to do it.

Praying the names of Christ, (whom John 1, 1 John 1 and Revelation 19:13 calls the WORD or Logos), from His Revealed Word – the Bible – will remove any doubt, anything to worry about or any reason to stomp and pout.

Live as if the power of Christ reigns in you. You will never regret it. It will take you out of the Danger Zone! As the lyrics to the songs says above "you will never know what you can do, until you get it up as high as you can go"! The Power of Christ is as HIGH as any mortal can go! Amen and amen!

2 Persistent Perseverance

"Energy and persistence conquer all things."[1]
Benjamin Franklin

One of the great founding fathers of this country was Ben Franklin. His accomplishments are part of American life. Most of us do not know the extent to which our everyday life was affected by this man, whose energy and curiosity was limitless. Here is a short list of some of the things Franklin "discovered", which we take for granted today:

1. Bi-focals (after his eyesight deteriorated).
2. Scuba diving (when he was 11 in 1717, he invented swimming fins).
3. Discovered how electricity works and the everyday use of it.
4. Discovered how to protect or ground your home from lightning (with his lightning rod).
5. Created the first lending library in America (the Library Company of America).
6. Created the first Mutual Insurance Company in America in 1751.
7. Created the first political cartoon (the PLAIN TRUTH publication of 1747)

He also wrote ""If you would not be forgotten as soon as you are dead & rotten, either write things worth reading, or do things worth the writing."[2]

---

[1] http://thinkexist.com/quotations/perseverance.
[2] www.geocities.com/bioelectrochemistry/franklin.htm.

What a mind and what energy from this man who lived the way he believed – free and libertine. Yet, for all his greatness and influence on modern American life, this worldly genius was a rebel against God and the Lord Jesus Christ. Nevertheless, even though he was a confirmed deist and freemason, Franklin supported the free exercise of religion and unknowingly had a major influence on the First Great Awakening, which began the spread Christianity deep inside known America of the period (1730's-1740).

British evangelist George Whitefield was so popular that thousands would come out to hear him preach, across the colonies. While Franklin was not a believer in Christ, he was so impressed with the English preacher and his ability to speak to up to 30,000 in public and then 20 people in a room, that Franklin became his main supporter![3]

Many biographies and Christian history books have recorded this fact. Franklin financed most of Whitefield's tracts and journals.[4] This enabled him to spread the Gospel all over many of the Colonies and sow the new birth of freedom for the great country that soon broke way from Whitefield's own England! Whitefield died in Massachusetts in 1770 before American Independence.

Americans love a great story of perseverance and/or rags to riches. This is why each year; the Horatio Alger Award arouses interest in its winner. Horatio Alger was a former Unitarian minister and is a story of redemption after a sex scandal. He went on to write over 100 books or novels on "sheer determination and good works" and how ANYONE can succeed in this great country, the land of opportunity.[5]

---

[3] Ibid.
[4] Ibid.
[5] http://www.enotes.com/history-fact-finder/economics-business/what-horatio-alger-story.

DANGER ZONE

Great stories of perseverance and persistence dot the early American landscape and have contributed to this country being the economic and military super power it has been for over 100 years. Failure is the pre-requisite to ultimate success. The precious diamond gem is actually a lump of coal that has been pressed and stressed over a long period of time. One man who kept failing was Thomas Alva Edison, the founder of the movie projector and other things, well, like the light bulb! It is amazing to me that people such as Franklin, Edison and others were such practical atheists. In fact, Edison once said "When a man is dead, he is dead! My mind is incapable of conceiving such a thing as a soul. I may be in error, and man may have a soul; but I simply do not believe it."[6]

His story of perseverance can only come from a God-given talent yet, he, like most successful men, rejected the Creator who gives us those gifts. Edison was pulled out of school by his parents after his teachers called him "stupid and unteachable"! Presumably, he was homeschooled. He went on to invent the light bulb and had 1093 patents. Even after his ore-mining plant in Ogdensburg, New Jersey failed to accomplish what he wanted, his patents in this plant revolutionized both the cement industry and the Assembly plant concept. Henry Ford (another non-believer) credited Edison with the concept for his Model T assembly lines.[7]

One thing to note here is the common thread of both Franklin and Edison. Both men were influenced by another atheist Thomas Paine. Franklin was a contemporary as we know from our history books since Paine was the intellectual power behind the America revolution with his pamphlet "Common Sense". Pamphlets back then were the equivalent of blogs today.

---

[6] http//www.hyperhistory.net/apwh/bios/b4edisont.htm#return1.
[7] http://www.growthink.com/content/7-entrepreneurs-whose-perseverance-will-inspire-you.

Americans have always had the genius of communication. History tells us Paine was not just a deist but a European-styled atheist in the "age of reason". It was Paine's writings that helped to turn Edison away from God.[8]

This is a warning to the people of God. If He is not the center of your very existence, nothing you do will matter at the point of your passing. Sure, there will be a legacy of great inventions which make life easier for millions, but where are Franklin and Edison today in eternity?

REFINER'S FIRE

Malachi 3: 2-3a (NLT) says "But who will be able to endure it when He comes? Who will be able to stand and face Him when he appears? For He will be like a blazing fire that refines metal, or like a strong soap that bleaches clothes. He will sit like a refiner of silver, burning away the dross".

Malachi's prophesy is about the coming and great day of the Lord Jesus, in all His Glory. However, it is important to note, for this discussion, the refining process. For precious metal to be classified as 99.9% pure, it has to go through fire, over and over again. I have never seen an ad for "100% pure" silver or gold…another testament to the fallen nature of creation, which still groans for the coming day of the Lord! For us to be used by God, after we are saved and justified is to be purified and sanctified!

Here is what 1 Peter 1:6-7 (NLT) says "So be truly glad. There is wonderful joy ahead, even though you have to endure many trials for a little while. These trials will show that your faith is genuine. It is being tested as fire tests and purifies gold— though your faith is far more precious than mere gold. So when your faith remains strong through many trials, it will bring you

---

[8] http://www.hyperhistory.net/apwh/bios/b4edisont.htm#return1

much praise and glory and honor on the day when Jesus Christ is revealed to the whole world".

These are horrible and critical days for everyone. However, for the Christian, how we conduct ourselves and persevere through them will reveal our true Christian character. The man or woman of God will not go unscathed through these evil days. A time will come, and is here for many in the body (especially in more oppressed countries) where we will be called to make a stand for Christ. Now is not the time to go weak in the knees or sell out as some were planning to do in the book of Hebrews, by returning to "the Law".

Christ warned as much many times. What he said can be paraphrased in these words – "I beg your pardon, I didn't promise you a rose garden." If the eternal Son of God could lay down His Life, be beaten, scorned and persecuted for His Kingdom, what makes us think we will escape tribulation and trials in this life? He did not give us a rose garden, but He gave us roses. The rose is at the top. Down the stem, we can be stuck with thorns, because thorns are part of the makeup of the rosebush.

Trials and tribulation can be two distinct protocols. In order to be totally official about this, the United States National Institutes of Health describes a protocol, in part, as an "action plan that describes what will be done in the study, how it will be conducted."[9]

Both trials and tribulation really are action plans. However, in my opinion, they sources are different. The Protocol of the trial can be instituted by God Himself. See the refining fire process from Malachi 3:2-3a.

A trial can come in any form. The most extreme on found in the Bible is, of course, Job. If someone were to tell Job, that Satan accused Job of being only loyal to God because God had protected Job and blessed him tremendously, so God told Satan to

---

[9] http://www.nlm.nih.gov/services/ctprotocol.html.

"go ahead and test him, just don't kill him," can you imagine?!! In our lifetime, we can have similar trials and afflictions.

Someone may get a bad report from the doctor about a potential terminal illness. I have known people who heard their young adult children died in accidents or got pregnant. Most of them are not Christians. We all know people who were laid off, or were missionaries in bad places, or were and are being ridiculed for their Christian beliefs. How do we make it through, even the next hour, in these situations?

Are their action plans, protocols to handle these? Sure there are. The obvious human reactions can be found in Job again. To paraphrase – Job whined and made up stories about God, while listening to stupid know-it-all friends! Sound familiar?! To make it worse, his own wife, whom God had given him, instructed him to "curse God and die"! At least she did not laugh like her distant cousin, Sarah, when Jesus told Abraham; he would have a son at 99 years old!

In the space of ten weeks, I was taken into emergency surgery and told the problem returned and if it were not taken care of, another abscess would result. In early March, an abscess in the perineum area was, maybe, a day short of permanently endangering my life as it was close to reaching my blood stream. God alone protected me.

I had ignored it when it was the size of a small cherry, thinking it was a boil that would go away. In four days, the small cherry-like growth was a six square inch abscess. In less than 1 hour at the doctor, I had gone from one end of town to a specialist to Memorial Hospital pre-op for emergency surgery.

A three-inch deep, fast moving abscess had to be drained out of me and a full bag of strong anti-biotics pumped in to kill the infection and 100-degree plus fever! The recovery time with a Seton tube sticking in me, and several baths per day, was very sobering and humbling. Never once did I blame the Lord or take pity on myself. I had learned the lesson of Job and many years of growing through trials and afflictions. One thing about being tested by the Lord that has served me well. When tough personal times come, and they will, we either go through them with Grace the first time, and stay firmly grounded in His Word and Truth, or the next trial will be tougher.

TO PERSEVERE: The Premise

Just walk in any Barnes and Noble, Borders and sadly, any Christian bookstore and the first thing you will see is a plethora of self-help books – most not based on anything Biblical. On the secular side, we can thank Oprah Winfrey for the rush of feel-good processes to handle what ails the human soul. On the "religious" side, things are no better. Almost every Christian "self-help" book starts off by telling you about God having a plan for your life….then goes into navel-gazing! Most of the authors are really into self-help – theirs!

As a mortal man, I know what a no-good, insufficient human being I was before Christ saved me. Even the slow process of sanctification leaves a lot of me to be desired in the eyes of the Lord. Like the Apostle Paul.

To know how to live outside the box of post-modern "Christianity" and the corrupt world systems, we have to see what God says about us. Christian women and men should not care what the world thinks of us. What is more significant is – What does God think about me?

Therefore, the premise we operate on, before going deep and comprehending God's prescription can be found in Romans 7: 14b-15 (NLT) "The trouble is with me, for I am all too human, a slave to sin. I do not really understand myself, for I want to do what is right, but I do not do it. Instead, I do what I hate".

Precisely! How can a human, who still has a sin nature (as long as we remain alive on earth), really comprehend what happened in Genesis 3 in the Garden of Eden! We are slaves to sin ….and not just the so-called Seven Deadly Sins but little ones like "little white lies," impatience with disobedient kids or intolerance of other Christians at times.

The thing is, we really do want to do what is right, but the Adamic sin nature in us prevents it. We certainly do not go into self-loathing, as we are saints by calling. We are more than conquerors. Even in our affliction, God expects us to live in that victory.

Apostle Paul was a man who was taken up to where Christ lives – the Third Heaven. He raised the dead, healed the sick, and cast out demons. Yet even he went on to say in, continuing in Romans 7: 18- 20 (NLT) "And I know that nothing good lives in me, that is, in my sinful nature. I want to do what is right, but I cannot. I want to do what is good, but I do not. I do not want to do what is wrong, but I do it anyway. But if I do what I don't want to do, I am not really the one doing wrong; it is sin living in me that does it".

There is one caveat. Paul did not say the "devil made me do it!" He is too much a man of Christ to bring the devil into our conversation. It is our fleshly nature.

Therefore, here in brief is the premise we proceed on when called upon to persevere through a hard period or process. The stress and fatigue of these evil times play havoc on our families, churches, jobs and communities. Our children face a bad future saddled by debt, moral relativism and a shrinking remnant in the true church. Taxes are high, crime is high, the very cost of daily living has skyrocketed and opportunity is shrinking. Who would have thought you would see college graduates and their wives moving back home into mom and dad's basement with their kids.

The economy is shrinking; jobs are going overseas to the global markets and on and on. The safe sanctuaries of the past are not safe anymore. As a result, we are stressed out, burnt out and just plain old out of energy. Some of the best-selling medications in America are anti-depressants.

- Is this how the Christian is supposed to live?
- Is this how are supposed to lead our families?
- Is this the kind of leadership we provide at home, church and work?
- Is this the legacy we are leaving our children?
- Is this the kind of testimony we should be showing a lost and dying world?

TO PERSEVERE: The Promise

Perseverance is a process, under the protocol of personal trials. Tribulation is another story. Most Americans have not been persecuted for their faith, at least not yet. However, days are coming, declares the Lord, when we will be hated MORE for believing and preaching the Name of Christ. Already pastors and ministers in Canada, our closest neighbor and friend, are arrested for preaching against the sin of Homosexuality. Most of us would not last a day in parts of Africa, India, Pakistan, China, Europe and other third world countries where Christ is so hated they burn churches and murder Christians ad hominem.

All over America, biblical or "orthodox" Christianity is under mortal attack. Our enemy, Satan, knows his days are increasingly numbered, so he is working overtime with those who not only openly follow the world, but those in the church who are asleep or could care less.

In fact, biblical teaching and mentoring are so woefully deficient in our churches, that the majority of Christian does not know the Bible has God's answers for everything that ails His people! The sufficiency of Holy Scripture has been replaced by out of context topical quotes, used to make people feel good in their current state. "All Scripture is God-breathed and is useful for teaching, rebuking, correcting and training in righteousness, so that the man of God may be thoroughly equipped for every good work" (2 Timothy 3:16-17, NIV).

Survey after survey, year after year, shows the biblical worldview of most Christians shrinking to less than 20% for adults to less than 10% for teens and young adults and sad. Romans 5: 1-5 has the attributes we need to make it through both trials and the coming tribulation of the saints.

First, we have the premise, as described in the previous section (that we are predisposed to act a certain way). However, Christ did not leave us there. Through the Apostle Paul in Romans 5, the Lord clearly shows we are more than qualified to make it through affliction, adversity and annoyances.

Romans 5: 1-5 (NKJV) says:

> Therefore, having been justified by faith, we have[a] peace with God through our Lord Jesus Christ, through whom also we have access by faith into this grace in which we stand, and rejoice in hope of the glory of God. And not only that, but we also glory in tribulations, knowing that tribulation produces perseverance; and perseverance, character; and character, hope. Now hope does not disappoint, because the love of God has been poured out in our hearts by the Holy Spirit who was given to us.

ATTRIBUTES OF THE CHRISTIAN WHO PERSEVERES

The word persevere comes from the Latin, meaning "to see (you) through. God has revealed the following attributes the Christian possesses to see us through these difficult personal and corporate issues:

1. From Romans 5: 1, we have an Inner Peace
2. From Romans 5: 2, we have access to Father God.
3. From Romans 5: 3, we have Hope in the Glory of God.

4. From Romans 5: 3, we have a calling to glory in tribulations.
5. From Romans 5: 4, we have a visible inner steadfastness of Hope.
6. From Romans 5: 5, we have a blessed assurance from God's love.
7. From Romans 5: 5, we have the Holy Spirit.

Inner Peace:

We see in during a high stressed situation like the terrorists attacks of 911. I remember that strange, silent morning when we realized everything America stood for – free enterprise, democracy, military strength and freedom, was under deadly attack by barbarians with a 7th century mentality. All around us in one of the largest office buildings in Springfield, the Illinois State Capital, panic and fear kicked in. Yet several of us, God's people, calmly but concerned went about our business. Those uncertain few early hours of the attack, when no one knew how far this would go, were the most critical ones.

Yet God wove such a blanket of peace that it covered the way I looked at the attacks to handling the uncertainty, should WE be under attack in the capital city. This kind of peace is more than the absence of the kind of fear. It is not a fuzzy feeling or cheap emotion. It is "Eirene" (in the Greek), which is total rest with God! When Christ, through Apostle Paul, says we have that "Eirene" with God,

He also means we have returned to the Default settings – the original state of restoration with our Creator. This is the state of peace we were in when God walked in the cool of the afternoon, through the Garden. We are not sinless as Adam was, pre-Genesis 3, but the enmity between man and God is over, once we accept Christ as Lord and Savior and are rejuvenated.

One thing should always be at the forefront of our minds – because we are now Children of the Living God, we are UNDER

HIS PROTECTION! Sure, bad temporal things will happen to us. Some of our brethren will be persecuted to the point of losing their lives for Christ. Either way, the rewards in heaven are greater for persevering in these tribulations. No weapon formed against us will prosper. No demon has power over us. We have the Power of God living within us. If that does not give us rest, we need to go on a retreat with a Bible and some hymnal music or have a visitation from some fired up elders in the church!

Access and Hope:

The next attribute of our new defense mechanism is Access. The real body of Christ is not the big crowds you see in American mega-churches. It is a remnant here, a remnant there and all over the fruited plain and around the world.

The word Access actually has the connotation of free admission! Our ticket was paid for at the Cross. Now can you wrap your mind around this? The Eternal God of the Universe allows people like you and I to approach Him!

Words like "favor" and "privilege" come to mind! It is more than a privilege to be allowed in front of the Throne of God, daily or whenever we wish, yet most Christians not only take that for granted but have no idea, we are these special "backstage passes"! Again, this attribute only exists by Grace through Faith in Christ alone.

No other people – past, present or future – have this type of access to any god. First of all, the many "gods" of the world religions do not exist. The majority of mankind – past, present and future – unfortunately would not be in the kingdom of God. We stand in His Grace, having been created for His Glory. So when bad times hit, we must never lose sight of the bigger picture of WHY we are His and the REASON we are His – all for His Glory!

This is where our Hope comes from. This kind of Hope is more than just an expectation. The original meaning is a proactive confident anticipation with pleasure!

Can you believe Eternal God would give US mere mortals such a joy to look forward to! Can you find where man-made cults and religion promises this AND can deliver it?

The payoff of such pure, untarnished hope is we can persevere with a Blessed Assurance, Jesus is mine. The rest of Romans 5:2 can be paraphrased as "oh what a foretaste of Glory divine" – His Glory! Amen and amen."

Steadfast in Tribulations:

Romans 5: 3 tells us to "glory in tribulations". How do we comply and does it mean we act like Peter and John in Acts 4, when they were rejoicing that they were beaten for the cause of Christ?

The answer is – Yes and Yes! Learning to endure the difficult times of layoffs, high debt and kids in college is one thing. Learning to apply that knowledge is another matter.

To be steadfast means the man or woman of God is unshakeable, unmovable and unbendable IN FAITH, in the face of personal or other trials. We do not laugh in the face of danger, but we do not cry either!

We simply use these times, with FIRM RESOLVE, as an opportunity to show the true character of a soldier of Christ. The word "soldier" is chosen on purpose. We are in a war. Christ did not call us to a tea party. We look forward to the Marriage Supper of the Lamb (which is a real banquet), but this takes place ONLY in Heaven. On earth, we are in daily Spiritual Warfare. If the Christian is not, then we have another problem with rejuvenation.

High Visibility, the Story of Milton Hershey:

Romans 5:4 KJV says "...and patience experience and experience hope". The original Greek word for "experience" is "Dokime" and is the same as Character. It also means, trustworthiness, proof (as in proof of integrity), tested and true, among other things.

Everyone loves a good Hershey's chocolate bar. What would candy runs for our kids (and us) be without Hershey's kisses, Special Dark and Kit Kat?! Hershey, Pennsylvania and Hershey products are as American as Coca Cola. But was it always so?

Milton Hershey dropped out of school in 4th Grade and went to work as an apprentice for a candy maker in Lancaster, Pa. for four years. Then in 1876, he left to start his own candy business and failed after six hard years of trying. He moved to Denver, Co. and worked for many years with a confectioner who taught him how to make caramels with fresh milk.[10]

He later moved to New York City and started another candy business. This also failed. Milton persevered. He moved back to Lancaster, Pa. and started the Lancaster Caramel Company. The company succeeded and soon employed 1400 people!

During Chicago's 1893 World's Columbian Exposition, Hershey saw something that affected the American sweet tooth – milk chocolate! Adopting the Swiss delicacy, he developed his own classic chocolate and the company that became known as the Hershey Chocolate Company.

What gave Hershey, a grade school dropout the drive to press on was his faith. Yes, the man who built factories, schools, churches and an entire town – Hershey, Pa. – was a real man of Christ! Milton was raised on the Bible and held those beliefs all his life. You can see it by the way he cared for the people who worked for him.

---

[10] http://www.hersheys.com/discover/milton/milton.asp.

DANGER ZONE

In his own words, Hershey had these words for hard times "I believe that hard luck and misfortune are good for people. Therefore, you should take your problem as you asked for it, nay pray for it. Difficulties show men what they are."[11] However, it was his faith in the Word of God and Christ that make these words more impressive.

Hershey said "God speaks through men to speak the truth, our hands to do His work here below, voices and clean hands to make liberty and love prevail over injustice and hate. Without faith in our work and in ourselves, we cannot succeed in a long measure in life's undertaking. Without faith we cannot know our God and Creator…..I am a Christian in the only sense that Christ wished anyone to be, sincerely attached to his doctrine in preference to all other."[12]

Faith like this is not seen much in any part of corporate America, whether it is 100 years ago or now. Real Christian industrialists are so rare, we know their individual names! Hershey is the great American example of Perseverance, leading to Character, Hope and blessing.

All seven attributes of the Promise are rolled up in the story of this man. For the Christian, the most important of these attributes is the indwelling of the Holy Spirit. This is the only evidence ever that we are saved and redeemed by the Lord Jesus Christ. Without the Holy Spirit, the Process we have to go through in Trials and tribulations will be a meaningless exercise!

TO PERSEVERE: The Process

We have looked, in some depth, into the Premise of Perseverance, the Promise of Perseverance and now James, the

---

[11]http://www.miltonshershey.com/TheHersheys/ChatwithMiltonHershey/tabid/402/Default.aspx.
[12] Ibid.

half brother of Jesus, shows us the Process, wherein lies our authority to persevere. This amazingly humble chief of the Christian church in Jerusalem gives us the Five Tools we need to Persevere and Endure through the Trials. These tools give us the opportunity to put everything we have learned into action. The very same attributes Christ defined in us, through Paul in Romans 5: 1-5, qualify us to act as James prescribed! This is a mystery we can never hope to understand on this side of Heaven!

Verses 2-11 of James chapter 1 have the spirit of these tools and as if that were not enough, James then proceeds to give us Verse 12 as the payoff, if we make it through the Process! Praise His Great Name! James 1: 2-11 (NLT) says:

> Dear brothers and sisters, when troubles come your way, consider it an opportunity for great joy. For you know that when your faith is tested, your endurance has a chance to grow. So let it grow, for when your endurance is fully developed, you will be perfect and complete, needing nothing. If you need wisdom, ask our generous God, and he will give it to you. He will not rebuke you for asking. But when you ask him, be sure that your faith is in God alone. Do not waver, for a person with divided loyalty is as unsettled as a wave of the sea that is blown and tossed by the wind. Such people should not expect to receive anything from the Lord. Their loyalty is divided between God and the world, and they are unstable in everything they do. Believers who are poor have something to boast about, for God has honored them. And those who are rich should boast that God has humbled them. They will fade away like a little flower in the field. The hot sun rises and the grass withers; the little flower droops and falls, and its beauty fades away. In the same way, the rich will fade away with all of their achievements.

DANGER ZONE

The Weapons of Winning through Perseverance are:

1. A joyful attitude (verse 2)
2. An understanding mind (verse 3)
3. A submissive will (verse 4)
4. A believing heart (verses 5-8)
5. A humble spirit (verses 9-11)
6.

A Joyful Attitude:

Simply put, the Bible clearly shows the way to having an attitude dedicated to Christ. Here is what God says in Hebrews 12: 2-3 (NIV): "Let us fix our eyes on Jesus, the author and perfecter of our faith, who for the joy set before him endured the cross, scorning its shame, and sat down at the right hand of the throne of God. Consider him who endured such opposition from sinful men, so that you will not grow weary and lose heart".

Jesus, the Prince (real meaning of the word "author") who defined and completed the covenant on the Cross, showed us the very way!

He had the exceedingly great gladness of the Kingdom to come! He knew He had to endure persecution, hate, shame, scorn and a humiliating death on a Tree, in order to complete God's plan for the Coming New Paradigm.

His way is the only way to endure the Daily Cross. We are meant to take up the cross and follow Him (the requirements of being a disciple). The author ran the race Himself endured the shameful Cross)and having completed it, He now waits for the completion of the Church age for us to finish OUR race.

There are no off ramps or rest stops. This one narrow one lane highway has one green light. You are either on it, or you are not. Which is it?

One final thing about having the attitude of gratitude in trials is this – no matter what happens to us, God means it for our own ultimate good.

An Understanding Mind:

James 1: 3 tells us to comprehend the fact of a Faith Tested can lead to the capacity to endure and grow!

Here is the opportunity to prove we have learned from the Scriptures. Trials add Endurance to our faith that leads to a stretching of our faith. We will never know how firm or weak we are in Christ until we are forced, by a circumstance, to respond in a Christ-like manner.

Remember a diamond, that most precious of gems, begins as a lump of carbon coal. It must be placed under 435,113 pounds per square inch of pressure at approximately 752 degrees! This pressure (psi) and heat makes the diamond such an amazingly hardened gem that it can cut glass and is anywhere from 10 to 100 times harder than any other gem![13]

The man and woman of Christ can be this priceless jewel in this dark world. All we have to do is let our light shine, by living ABOVE our circumstances and not UNDER them, and be found an enduring example of trust and Faith.

- Endurance is the intended outcome of testing.
- Endurance is not sitting back and being passive but standing strong in the face of storms.
- Endurance develops the complete person who is strong and mature, not one who runs from difficult things or seeks escape in earthly mechanisms.

A Submissive Will:

---

[13] http://science.howstuffworks.com/diamond1.htm.

The King James Bible uses the word "patience" in James 1:4 as in "But let patience have her perfect work, that ye may be perfect and entire, wanting nothing".

The original word is Hupomone or patient waiting or enduring. This process can only be manifested to a will that is completely submitted to the Authority of His Will!

When we see our trials through His Eyes, it works! Consider the little chorus "God Will Take Care of You":

> No matter what may be the test,
> God will take care of you;
> Lean, weary one, upon His breast,
> God will take care of you.
>
> God will take care of you,
> Through every day, over all the way;
> He will take care of you,
> God will take care of you.

Patient waiting or leaning on Him is more than a cliché it is real. So many Scriptures speak to those who are submitted to and wait for His Timing. Isaiah 40:31 (NASB) "Yet those who wait for the LORD will gain new strength; they will mount up with wings like eagles, they will run and not get tired, they will walk and not become weary".

Pearl B. Wait was not a very good cough syrup salesman in 1897, so he decided to sell food, door to door, would be a better prospect. There was this useless product called Gelatin. Wait came up with the idea to add corn syrup to it (later on his wife and him added a few flavor) and call it "Jell-O".[14]

Pearl B. Wait was just as horrible a salesman of Jell-O, as he was a cough syrup salesman. So in 1900, he sold the rights and

---

[14] http://www.ideafinder.com/history/inventions/jello.htm.

recipe for Jell-O for only $450! Jell-O went on to become the most popular dessert in the world![15] Pearl B. Wait just could not wait!

A Believing Heart:

The great prophet Jeremiah said the heart is exceedingly wicked, perverse, sick and evil (Jeremiah 17:9). This is the unsaved heart. At the same time, as we talked about earlier, we still have problems with sin. Even while writing this, the distractions are too numerous and need to be cut off!

What about the Spiritual Heart and how are we to refocus our spiritual hearts to combat depression, stress, frustration and everything else associated with surviving tests and trials.

Psalm 51:6 (AMP) has a key to what the Bible describes as the spiritual heart. It says "Behold, You desire truth in the inner being; make me therefore to know wisdom in my inmost heart".

Let's deconstruct this verse, as it contains the definition of the "inner being" or the real heart…the heart which God. The original Hebrew word is "tuwchah". In a physical sense, it means the Kidneys, the organs that purify the blood.

In the figurative and spiritual sense, the word means the inward thoughts. This is not just a mind game, but the processes of the mind that links to our emotions and actions.

Then "now wisdom" is from the Hebrew "yada"….or intimate knowledge of the "chokmah" or wise, wit and oracles of God. The book of Romans confirms God has revealed some of His Mysteries to mortal men.

The use of the word "heart" in the verse is from the Hebrew word "catham" or the "secret place"!

What is so marvelous about the Word of God is – it means what it says! Investigating the Truth of the Bible is relatively easy

---

[15] Ibid.

once we go phrase by phrase or word by word. Any attempt to interpret the Bible in human strength is called "allegory" and that stands in absolute error.

We have to guard against the typical small group or Sunday School bible study which, more and more, seems to descend to "what does this verse MEAN TO YOU"! The real question is "what is God saying here"!

Therefore, Psalm 51:6 reveals the Spiritual heart is the innermost secret place where we instinctively and intuitively can know the revelation of God, as revealed to the Christian, through the Holy Spirit.

We either believe He is able to complete it, through our trials, or we do not. There is no middle ground to the Believing Heart. We must seek the Wisdom of God in these trying times of economic, social and spiritual crisis.

Divine wisdom is the common sense of mortal men. This is commonly called "head knowledge". As we know, even the demons "know" truth such as, Jesus being the Son of God! Why do we constantly think we can lean on our own understanding? Proverbs 3: 5 says "trust in the Lord with ALL your heart"….not just some of it.

I have tried this "leaning on my own understanding" thing, and it got me nowhere – fast! We have to detach ourselves completely from our own selves, to receive this Divine wisdom and then execute this revelation.

Look at Proverbs 3: 6-7 (AMP) "In all your ways know, recognize, and acknowledge Him, and He will direct and make straight and plain your paths. Be not wise in your own eyes; reverently fear and worship the Lord and turn [entirely] away from evil."

- A believing heart knows the Savior.
- A believing heart recognizes His Omnipotence.
- A believing heart therefore bows to His Majesty.

Due to a believing heart, the Lord will direct us out of the paths of evil, sickness, debt, unemployment, family problems, pornography and all the other problems of modern life.

The verse says to fear and worship the Lord. If we keep our eyes on WHO He is, thereby putting Him IN FRONT of our circumstances, problems look a lot more manageable in His Light. I can not help but think if Job had that "yada" or true knowledge of the Holy, half of the book of Job would not exist. With Christ, we are already ahead of where Job was.

A Humble Spirit:

The rest of this awesome passage in James (verses 9-11) really shows the wonderful heart of the half-brother of the Lord Jesus.

The Amplified Version really takes away a long expository explanation: "Let the brother in humble circumstances glory in his elevation [as a Christian, called to the true riches and to be an heir of God], and the rich [person ought to glory] in being humbled [by being shown his human frailty], because like the flower of the grass he will pass away. For the sun comes up with a scorching heat and parches the grass; its flower falls off and its beauty fades away. Even so will the rich man wither and die in the midst of his pursuits".

Even in trials, the humble brother or sister in Christ should:

- Consider the lowly and poor.
- Consider the persecuted church in other countries.
- Consider the eternal state.

Wealth can not save you. The perfect example is the rich man in hell and Lazarus in the bosom of Abraham. This is not a story, it is real. It does not mean ALL rich people are lost or all poor people are saved. God uses all stations of temporal life to accomplish His eternal Will.

As American Christians, what James calls us to do, is not concentrate on the air-conditioned comfort or our clean, beautiful pews and sound systems, but outside the four walls of the average church.

This is where the real hurt and need is. This is where the mission field should be, not inside the church building, to where the mission fields has unfortunately has spread.

The Reward for Perseverance:

Finally, the brother of Jesus the Savior, in James 1:12 tells us what the reward for making it through fires of trials and tribulations are. The book of Job tells us how God rewarded Job for his faithfulness (see Job 42: 10-17).

James 1:12 (AMP): "Blessed (happy, to be envied) is the man who is patient under trial and stands up under temptation, for when he has stood the test and been approved, he will receive [the victor's] crown of life which God has promised to those who love Him."

3 Leaving a Living Legacy

> *"What you leave behind is not what is engraved in stone monuments, but what is woven into the lives of others."*
> Pericles, General of Athens,
> ruler of Tyre (495-429BC)

To the secular world and even some professing Christians, the Bible is an ancient book of stories and creeds that have no bearing on modern life in the western world! This is so woefully wrong, yet the emphasis on discipleship and biblical knowledge is missing completely in action in most "evangelical" churches.

The latest surveys from reputable polling companies in American have found that somewhere between 4% and 5% of Americas even claim to have a biblical Worldview! This is incredible in its magnitude and shows just how far the church in the West (Europe and the American Continent) has fallen into a pit, called the total depravity of man.

A worldview is the foundation whose parameters are set and defined by a set of doctrines. These doctrines then define the precise view of God, Christ, the Holy Spirit, Salvation, Grace and so on. A biblical worldview involves mortals like us realizing that the chief end of man is to Glorify and serve God.

While D.L. Moody and others were transforming America and the world with the Third Great Awakening, the seeds of apostasy were being sowed both in America and Great Britain. Western Europe abandoned Christ centuries before. Despite the great Welch Revival of 1904 led by Evan Roberts, Britain slid quickly into decadence.

Over the last century, the western church became more about programs and navel-gazing and music than the actual work Christ gave us to do. That work still is to "go into the entire world and make disciples".

Disciples leave legacies. We are having a smaller remnant of true disciples of Jesus these days, because both men and women have come to view church as therapy rather than an extension of their own worship of God, the other 6 days and 23 hours of the week.

When you add the lack of proper discipleship in almost every church I have been to or know of, it is small wonder that Ken Ham and Britt Beemer discovered the most extensive and damaging, distressing news of the past few years about our churches.

In the recent book ALREADY GONE, both Ham and Beemer found we have already lost the next generation of believers in kids Sunday School! Our well meaning Sunday school teachers and their wonderful Bible stories and the way they are taught mean nothing to children who are fed the opposite in schools the rest of the week.

Children as young as 6th grade have already tuned out these well –known bible stories they have heard since pre-school, because the church is not teaching them HOW those stories apply to their lives!

They are not taught in church to defend the gospel. There is no emphasis on prayer, which brings the revelation and discernment to the teaching of the Word. Then at home, the bible stays on the shelf.

Parents themselves have no way of passing on the Knowledge of God, which our parents passed on to us, because they were not taught themselves! They were never taught to be disciples!

Legacy is important as you will read in the rest of this chapter. What we pass on to the next generation is a Biblical command. Whether modern professing Christians and evangelical churches believe it or not, EVERY syllable of the Word of God, is spirit-breathed and written by the Very Hand of God, using man as His instrument.

This command from Deuteronomy 11:19 (NASB) is more relevant today than when the LORD GOD Himself gave it to Moses. Here is what He says "You shall teach them [the Words of the LORD] to your sons and daughters, talking of them when you sit in your house and when you walk along the road and when you lie down and when you rise up".

Examine yourself; are we doing precisely this, as an announced people of God? Are we using every opportunity as a teachable moment to show the Goodness, grace and power of God? Are we?

In this chapter, I examined Jacob's (Israel's) final words and statements to his sons and followed each son through Biblical History to see how they fared. You see, Legacy, starts with final words as final blessings are still more important today than your next Tweet on Twitter of status update on Facebook!

It is amazing how Jacob's blessings led to each son fulfilling destinies which, most of the time, were not glorifying of God whatsoever! Please keep reading the chapter, because there are some wonderful American examples, some of which I discovered myself while researching this section. In fact, I am still friends with a descendant of Edward Wightman – Ron, whose side of the family joined the Mormon Church over 150 years ago!

Each of the sons (who became the Twelve Tribes of Israel) has a final statement from Genesis 49, as pronounced by their father Jacob on his deathbed. Then we follow the son/tribe briefly through the Scriptures, to see what happened to them. It was a very interesting exercise!

JACOB AND THE TWELVE TRIBES

In Genesis 49, verse 1-28, we read a stunning blessing pronounced by a dying Jacob upon his twelve sons. Many years after reuniting with his son Joseph in the Land of the Pharaohs, Jacob (Israel) brings down a hammer on the heads of most of his sons as he prepares to die. Ten of his twelve sons had caused him pain.

Most of them had violated many of the statutes of the Holy God of Abraham, Isaac and Jacob, even if the Law of Moses would not be given for almost 500 years! The following account of the sons and the blessings from their dying father is significant for its course change in human history.

There is application to us Gentiles across the spectrum of the past 4500 years. Many people today think God is asleep because He may not punish us for our sins right away, "therefore He must be looking the other way, and it is alright to continue in this sin!" Not so, my friend. What the world and its followers are actually doing is storing up Wrath for themselves, on the Day of Judgment, unless they are washed CLEAN by the Blood of the Lamb!!

With this in mind, here are the blessings on each of the sons of Jacob and what became of them, over time.

REUBEN (Genesis 49: 3-4a) NKJV

Reuben, you are my firstborn, my might and the beginning of my strength, the excellency of dignity and the excellency of power. Unstable as water, you shall not excel, because you went up to your father's bed; then you defiled ... (with Jacob's wife Bilhah) (Reference: Genesis 35:22)

The issue with Rueben applies to a lot of Christians (and non-Christians sometimes). We may not do vile things. We may be impetuous and full of vigor and virtue, but if there is an unconfessed sin in our lives, all of that means absolutely nothing to a Holy God. Reuben had tried to save Joseph from being murdered by his other brothers. The sin of Adultery against God, and the curse upon him from Jacob ("you shall not excel"), eventually led to this tribe being wiped out in Israel when the Syrian King Tiglath-Pileser captured them and the half tribe of Manasseh (1 Chronicles 5:26).

DANGER ZONE

Not surprisingly, the Reubenites TOTALLY abandoned the faith of the God of Abraham, Isaac and Jacob. Not one prophet, judge or hero came from this first son of Jacob…NOT ONE!

SIMEON AND LEVI (Genesis 49: 5-7) NKJV

Simeon and Levi are brothers; instruments of cruelty are in their dwelling place. Let not my soul enter their council; let not my honor be united to their assembly; for in their anger they slew a man (Reference Genesis 34:24-26), and in their self-will they hamstrung an ox. Cursed be their anger, for it is fierce; and their wrath, for it is cruel! I will divide them in Jacob and scatter them in Israel.

Most of us will never let our discontent, even anger, rise to such a point that double-cross and premeditated murder (the entire chapter of Genesis 34) result. But thinking such thoughts are just as evil. Jesus preached many times against the sin of the mind (anyone who looks at a woman with lust for her has already committed adultery with her in his heart… Matt.5:28). Simeon and Levi dishonored their father by this vile murderous act. They brought the Wrath of God upon their own heads, even though the Levite tribe produced some notable Biblical stalwarts.

The Simeonites faded away and blended into the pagan Northern Kingdom of Israel, fulfilling the prediction of God through Jacob, in verse 26. 1 Chronicles 4: 41-43 reveals what a useless, Godless people they had become, just like Simeon, the father of that tribe. There was nothing more abominable in the sight of God that the Northern Kingdom.

Levi's descendants (the Levites) were of no major account until the time of Moses and his brother Aaron. God Himself chose the Levites out of the Twelve to be His priests and minister in the Tabernacle and later Temple. He consecrated them unto Himself and gave specific instructions for their conduct.

Aaron, the first priest of Israel, almost set the tone for the Levites later on in their awful rebellious history. He did so right from the beginning. In Exodus 32, while Moses was up on the Mountain of God getting the Law from the Hand of the LORD, Aaron was making a golden pagan calf to pacify the ungrateful mob. In verse 32, he blamed the people, even though the calf was HIS idea! Then he said "I threw the gold into the fire and OUT CAME THIS CALF!" (Verse 24). But Moses, writing in Verse 35 said "God smote them…..because of the calf Aaron had made". I suspect Aaron will be held responsible for that on the Day of Wrath! When will God's people ever learn!

The Levites engaged in vile abominations at times, just like their Tribal Father Aaron. From the sons of Eli (1 Samuel 2:11-13) to the Pharisees and Scribes of the New Testament, they are shining examples of disobedience and total violation of the Word of God.

The Chosen Prophet Jeremiah was the son of the Levite Priest Hilkiah who was part of the corrupt priestly system during the reigns of Kings Jehoiakim and Zedekiah. Both these kings had pagan gods in their palaces and bowed down to them, all the while claiming they worshipped the one true God of Israel! The priests went along with their rulers in this corruption.

In Ezekiel, the house of Israel was so vile, the priests were committing abominations right in the temple!

Jesus Himself scolded Nicodemus in John 3: 10 (Jesus answered and said to him, "Are you the teacher of Israel and do not understand these things?) The Levites themselves were condemned to Hell by Jesus. I would urge the reading of the entire Chapter of Matthew 23 for context!

The Pharisees and high priests of the Temple were so caught up in their man-made traditions and "rule on rule, rule on rule….a little here and a little there" (from Isaiah 28:13) they could not discern the prophesies of their own prophets. By the way, these are the same Prophets they murdered or exiled!

So the heritage of these Simeon and Levi is significant, to the larger context of the God's Original plan. The application the LORD wants us to take from this, as mothers and fathers, is "actions have consequences". It is so easy to fall from Grace if one is not careful. But more important than this is the Lord has a warning in Luke 12: 48 "But he who did not know, yet committed things deserving of stripes, and shall be beaten with few. For everyone to whom much is given, from him much will be required; and to whom much has been committed, of him they will ask the more."

Jesus had this warning for the descendants – the Scribes and Pharisees - of the Levite priests in Matthew 23 NIV who were about to kill Him for speaking God's Truth:

> You snakes! You brood of vipers! How will you escape being condemned to hell? Therefore, I am sending you prophets and wise men and teachers. Some of them you will kill and crucify; others you will flog in your synagogues and pursue from town to town. And so upon you will come all the righteous blood that has been shed on earth, from the blood of righteous Abel to the blood of Zechariah son of Berekiah, whom you murdered between the temple and the altar. I tell you the truth; all this will come upon this generation.

These men, placed in a high position by God, through the Levitical priesthood even as it was coming to a close due to the New Covenant of Christ, bore the blood of Isaiah, Zechariah, John the Baptist and other Old Testament prophets on their hands. They did not actually commit these acts, but came from a murderous generation that did. The Key word here is Legacy. Blood guilt and damnation was their legacy.

Even as Aaron's rod, which budded, lay in the Ark of the Covenant, his priesthood and God's covenant with his tribe is now history. We have a new High Priest forever and ever, and

His Name is Jesus. His is the True Legacy from the Father. The Twelve Tribes of Jacob have their symbolic place in the Kingdom of Heaven, as do the Patriarchs Abraham, Isaac and Jacob, but those actual members of the body of Israel are another story.

JUDAH

The blessing to Judah was stunning in its Messianic prophesy. Our Savior, Jesus Christ came from this line and is known as the Lion of Judah. Jacob's blessing, from the Amplified Bible, Genesis 49: 8-11 reads thus:

> Judah, you are the one whom your brothers shall praise; your hand shall be on the neck of your enemies; your father's sons shall bow down to you. Judah, a lion's cub! With the prey, my son, you have gone high up [the mountain]. He stooped down, he crouched like a lion, and like a lioness--which dares provoke and rouse him? The scepter or leadership shall not depart from Judah, nor the ruler's staff from between his feet, until Shiloh [the Messiah, the Peaceful One] comes to whom it belongs, and to Him shall be the obedience of the people. Binding His foal to the vine and His donkey's colt to the choice vine, He washes His garments in wine and His clothes in the blood of grape

It is fitting God took the Priesthood away from the corrupt, murderous Levites, and gave it permanently to His Son, from one Tribe to another! This legacy from Judah's line came about only because Jesus was the God-man! He was and still is the God who became man, identified with His Flock (us), died a real death on the Cross, and rose to the Father as our Intercessor. He could only be our Intermediary before the Father because of the Cross!!

DANGER ZONE

You wonder why liberal theologians and the world, doing the bidding of Satan, deny the Cross. They do because Jesus walked into Heaven after the Ascension, forty days post-Crucifixion, victoriously as permanent High Priest on our behalf! That is something NOBODY can take away for us! Hebrews 4:14-16 (AMP) reveals as much here:

> Inasmuch then as we have a great High Priest Who has [already] ascended and passed through the heavens, Jesus the Son of God, let us hold fast our confession [of faith in Him]. For we do not have a High Priest Who is unable to understand and sympathize and have a shared feeling with our weaknesses and infirmities and liability to the assaults of temptation, but One Who has been tempted in every respect as we are, yet without sinning. Let us then fearlessly and confidently and boldly draw near to the throne of grace (the throne of God's unmerited favor to us sinners), that we may receive mercy [for our failures] and find grace to help in good time for every need [appropriate help and well-timed help, coming just when we need it].

There is no underestimating how significant this fact is to the Believer in Jesus Christ. Even the other part of the Blessing to Judah in Verse 11 (He washes His garments in wine and His clothes in the blood of grapes) talks of the Lord when He returns in Glory to take down the secular kings of the earth in Revelation 19:13 with the Armies of Heaven dressed in white linen on white horses.

This prophecy from the dying Jacob wraps up in this verse from Revelation 19:13 "He was clothed with a robe dipped in blood, and His name is called The Word of God". Jesus as our Savior/High Priest means not only His confession of our name on Judgment Day but as Intercessor to our prayers on this side of Heaven!

There are many other things to be written on this topic but for now, suffice it to say, this blessing to Judah, is the most important of the Twelve by Jacob to his sons. Here are the other blessings, briefly and how the Tribes fared in the annals of history.

ZEBULON; ISSACHAR; DAN

Genesis 49:13, AMP: Zebulun shall live toward the seashore, and he shall be a haven and a landing place for ships; and his border shall be toward Sidon.

Zebulon was an obscure son. He almost faded into the shades of history except for one big mention in the Book of Judges. His tribe fought valiantly alongside Naphtali's tribe and was mentioned by the Judge Deborah in Judges 5:18.

Genesis 49:14,15, AMP: Issachar is a strong-boned donkey crouching down between the sheepfolds and he saw that rest was good and that the land was pleasant; and he bowed his shoulder to bear [his burdens] and became a servant to tribute [subjected to forced labor].

Issachar's tribe settled in some of the richest land in the land of Palestine, at the time, just as Jacob predicted! They were not noted for much else, except being hardworking farmers!

Genesis 49: 16, 17, AMP: Dan shall judge his people as one of the tribes of Israel. Dan shall be a serpent by the way, a horned snake in the path that bites at the horse's heels, so that his rider falls backward.

Samson and the Judges of Israel came from the Tribe of Dan (see the entire Book of Judges). One of God's greatest Generals was the great Gideon, a Danite. In 1 Chronicles 2:12, Dan is omitted and in Revelation 7. The Angel of Heaven left Dan out of the 144,000 saved out of the Tribulation by Jesus, at the End times!

GAD; ASHER; NAPHTALI

Genesis 49: Gad--a raiding troop shall raid him, but he shall raid at their heels and assault them [victoriously].

The name Gad means "a troop". His tribe was vicious and warlike. They moved to East of the Jordan and occupied part of the mountainous area, intermingling with the Ammonites. However, 12,000 of them were sealed by the Angel of God in Revelation 7, of the 144,000...as were 12,000 of each tribe EXCEPT Dan!

Genesis 49: 20, AMP: Asher's food [supply] shall be rich and fat, and he shall yield and deliver royal delights.

Asher also settled into rich farm land in Palestine. They lived very close to the Mediterranean coast.

Genesis 49: 21, AMP: Naphtali is a hind let loose which yields lovely fawns.

The tribe of Naphtali was recorded fighting valiantly alongside Zebulon in the book of Judges.

JOSEPH AND BENJAMIN

Genesis 49: 22-26, AMP:

Joseph is a fruitful bough, a fruitful bough by a well (spring or fountain), who do branches run over the wall. Skilled archers have bitterly attacked and sorely worried him; they have shot at him and persecuted him. But his bow remained strong and steady and rested in the Strength that does not fail him, for the arms of his hands were made strong and active by the hands of the Mighty God of Jacob, by the name of the Shepherd, the Rock of Israel, by the God of your father, Who will help you, and by the Almighty, Who will bless you with blessings of the heavens above, blessings lying in the deep beneath, blessings of the breasts and of the womb.

The blessings of your father [on you] are greater than the blessings of my forefathers [Abraham and Isaac on me] and are as lasting as the bounties of the eternal hills; they shall be on the head of Joseph, and on the crown of the head of him who was the consecrated one and the one separated from his brethren and [the one who] is prince among them.

The tribe of the great Joseph, Prime Minister of Egypt, was split into Ephraim and Manasseh. Ancient Jewish Tradition says Joseph wanted to have reconciliation with his brothers after Jacob's death, something Jacob did not bless him with. Like the first time, tradition says, his brothers double-crossed him again. Joseph himself was a blessed man and his bones were buried right next to Jacob's well, until it was desecrated in 2005 AD by Palestinian guerrillas. His tribes later split.

However, these tribes are also sealed by the Angel of God in Revelation 7, while Ephraim and Dan are left out! Both Joseph and his sub-tribe are mentioned as saved by the Spirit. Dan was accountable for introducing worship of worthless pagan gods and idols.

Genesis 49: 27, AMP: Benjamin is [a] ravenous wolf, in the morning devouring the prey and at night dividing the spoil.

The Benjamites were a ferocious fighting lot. King Saul, the first king of Israel, came out of this tribe. They were eventually swallowed up by the Tribe of Judah and not heard from again in the rest of the Bible. Famous Benjamites were the Apostle Paul and Jonathan, friend of the great King David.

The reason for examining the Blessings of Jacob on his twelve sons to a certain depth was to provide the background for a Biblical understanding of Legacy. These are not just stories which occurred 3700 years ago in a vacuum, but events led by people who have impacted several millennia, cultures and everything up to this point in time.

An important thing to note here, is how much Jesus Christ is in the picture from Genesis to Revelation and what an outstanding presence He has even from the Blessing to Judah until the Sealing of the Tribes and the 144,000 evangelists who are the Remnant of the Tribes in the End times.

LEGACY-THE DEFINITION

Webster's Dictionary defines "legacy" as "something transmitted by or received from an ancestor or predecessor or from the past". What some of these men, Jacob's sons, transmitted was more than bad news. It was the worse news ever in terms of Eternity. Their lot was smeared with the foul mud of their pre-Egypt conduct and their uniting with Joseph again. But their deeds found them out right after both Jacob's and Joseph's deaths, as successive Pharaohs forgot the deeds of Joseph with the passage of time.

What are we transmitting to our children and future descendants? On our dying beds, what type of blessings would we confer on our surviving children? Are blessings like Jacob's even done today; in terms of its meaning of "formal approval"?

Proverbs 14:26: "He who fears the LORD has a secure fortress, and for his children it will be a refuge (NIV)." This is our battle cry and prerequisite as parents who can carry on the Biblical traditions of the great Patriarchs of Genesis!

But we do have a more modern example of a Jacob-like giant of the Faith, who has given us the example to be the kind of all-pro parents we should be, as we pass on to eternity. Read on!

THE LEGACY OF EDWARD WIGHTMAN, MARTYRED BY KING JAMES OF ENGLAND![16]

---

[16] The Reformed Reader,
http://www.reformedreader.org/history/christian/ahob2/chapter04.htm.

In the course of researching and seeking permission to use published materials concerning their family, I had the privilege of speaking to Ron Wightman. This fine gentleman currently lives in Salt Lake City, Utah and is a font of every knowledge concerning an American hero named Obadiah Holmes! I learnt something really important from him in the Legacy Line from Obadiah to Abraham Lincoln! Did I just say Abraham Lincoln, 16th President of these United States? Yes!

Ron told me about an important member of his family - Edward Wightman who was burnt at the stake in on April 11, 1612 by King James in England. This is the same King James after whom the KJV Bible is named! James was the keeper of the Church of England as the ruling monarch of Scotland and England. Edward was called a heretic because he was of the same Christian mindset as the Pilgrims who came over on the Mayflower!!

This simply meant he wanted the Freedom to worship God the way the Bible prescribed. One man, who did not come over to the U.S. but was persecuted by the English Church authorities around the same generation as Edward Wightman, was John Bunyan. We know him as the hero of the Faith who wrote Pilgrims Progress while in prison for preaching the Gospel Truth!

Edward was the last person ever burnt at the stake in England and is listed in Fox Book of Martyrs. His execution took place in Litchfield, England. History has it that as he was set ablaze by the king's henchmen, Edward screamed and said some seemingly unintelligible words.

The people nearby thought he was recanting his beliefs and put on the fire quickly! Then Edward began preaching the Gospel again and did what all good martyrs do – he stood firm on the Rock of Christ. They burnt him again.

The Wightman family still has his King James Bible in their prized possessions!

This historic family has bloodlines going all the way back to the founding of the Modern Christian church of America and its Baptist roots. For instance, one of the Martyred Edward's descendants is the Rev. Valentine Wightman whose line churched at Quidnessett Baptist Church.

His brother Daniel was co pastor of Second Baptist Church of Newport, Rhode Island. Any visitor to the super affluent Newport would not recognize its Christian heritage. It has fallen a long way from its innocent yet powerful God-inspired roots.

Now here is the reason Legacy is so important. Daniel's first wife was Susannah Holmes, granddaughter of the great Obadiah Holmes (see the rest of this chapter). Holmes was the pastor of First Baptist in Newport. Susannah's mother was Mary Sayles, the great-granddaughter of Roger Williams. Wightman family history calls Roger Williams (also see later on in this chapter) "that dauntless apostle of freedom of conscience."

Obadiah Holmes was one of the first Christian martyrs in the United States. A hero of the Baptist Faith, he was sentenced on May 31, 1651 for guess what – preaching and baptizing (by immersion) on the Lord's Day!! Holmes was born in Lancashire, England in 1607. He came to America like many Baptists, escaping persecution from those in the Church of England (whose current branch is the Episcopalian church of America).

Married to Katherine Hyde in 1646, Holmes was granted two acres in Salem, Massachusetts. A little known fact of history is he is the first man in America to manufacture glass!!

Most of the Baptists moved to the New York (then New Amsterdam) area to live around the Dutch, but Holmes settled in Massachusetts. The Pilgrims who lived in New England were Congregationalists who believed in Infant Baptism. This immediately caused a problem. By definition, Baptists believe in the Biblical form of Baptism.

(Infant Baptism comes out of theory from an early church father named Hippolytus in the 3rd Century who was the Bishop of Rome around 220. He was not a pope. The Apostle Peter was not the first pope of the Catholic Church either. This has been mythology passed down over centuries going back to Constantine in the 4th Century. Hippolytus inferred and basically created infant baptism out of whole cloth from earlier writings from the great martyr Polycarp, a friend of the Apostle John. There was wide disagreement over it and the controversy continues today.) 1

Obadiah Holmes found the same stringent old world practices from the protestant, yet Monarch-run Church of England, in the new American colonies. He rebelled.

His relative by marriage, Roger Williams, the founder of the Baptists in America, took a stand for the new Free Church in America against the Establishment (who had only a couple decades before come over on the Mayflower!). On November 13th 1644, an act was passed stating that any person who did not have their children 'sprinkled" (infant baptism), among other things, would face banishment.

Holmes was a teaching brother at the time. He was fined for acting like a real Baptist in the face of the same kind of persecution Martin Luther and others faced against the powerful Catholic Church, at the time of the reformation. A number of other brothers were arrested and fined for that "transgression". All the other men's fines were paid, but Holmes refused to have his paid, even though it was one of the heavier fines of thirty pounds, a huge amount in the 17th Century! So the Pilgrims, who fled England for religious freedom, had Obadiah flogged! 1

He was whipped in public so badly; he was unable to do anything except rest on his elbows and knees in jail…by the authorities! On behalf of religion! Holmes soon left Salem for Rhode Island where he became co-pastor of First Baptist Church of Newport.

By the way, the Congregationalist church which persecuted Holmes was started by the Pilgrims. It is now one of the most liberal churches in American and part of the extreme leftist denomination, the United Church of Christ. Salem is well known throughout American history for its famous 'witch trials'.

DANGER ZONE

On a parallel basis, Roger Williams was once the pastor in Salem. He moved to Plymouth and then back to Salem in 1635. He too ran into trouble with the church authorities in the colony for his 'radical behavior'! His now mainstream evangelical views were heresy to the governing authorities. They banished him from Salem. When he continued speaking out, the authorities came after him to send him to trial in England where he would have no doubt met the same fate as Martyr Edward Wightman.

Williams set out in a canoe with five other men and landed at a new settlement on the Moshassuck River. Because he said he got there by the "providence of God", he named the settlement Providence - now the capitol of Rhode Island.

During our three year stay in Hartford, Ct., my wife Vicki and I were members of the Immanuel Congregational Church, right across the street from Mark Twain's house where he wrote Huck Finn, Tom Sawyer and others! We spent most of our time in that church teaching the Bible to kids in the basement, while the service was going on upstairs. It was one of the biggest blessings of our lives. Most or all of them did not know what was in the Bible. The Lord brought several children to an initial knowledge of Him and we were able to see fruit in less than three years with the same kids. This was our mission in Hartford.

Apart from his persecution, a requisite for a true man of Christ, Obadiah Holmes is better known for what he did just before he died. His letter to his nine children is a masterpiece, still quoted in devotionals by many family ministries. It stands as a loving testimony of a father on his way to be with Jesus. Here are parts of his famous letter to his nine children, a treatise that will inspire you!

My Dear Children:[17]

---

[17] All information on the Wightman Family Heritage and Abraham Lincoln courtesy of Ronald Wightman (cousin to the Lincolns), Salt Lake City, Utah, www.wightmanfamily.com/holmes.html.

"A word or two unto you all who are near and dear unto me, and much on my heart as I draw near to my end and am not likely to see you nor speak to you at my departure. Wherefore I am moved to leave these lines for your consideration when I am gone and you shall see me no more.

Above all things in this world let it be your care to seek the Kingdom of Heaven and His righteousness first. Be you thoroughly convinced of that and, by actual transgressions, that you are sinners. Yet, know that such great love as cannot be expressed by man or angels has the Lord sent and held forth: even his Son, his only Son, to save and deliver you from wrath....

My soul has been in great trouble for you, to see Christ formed in you by a thorough work of the Holy Spirit of the Lord that it may appear you are born again and engrafted in the true vine; so you, being true branches, may bring forth fruit unto God and serve Him in your generation. Wherefore, wait on Him with care and diligence; carefully read the Scriptures and mind well what is therein contained, for they testify of Him."

Obadiah Holmes started his letter with the most important issue in life: repentance from sin and faith in Jesus Christ. He knew that if his descendants missed Christ then they would miss life. And now my son, Joseph: Remember that Joseph of Arimathea was a good man and a disciple of Jesus; he was bold and went in boldly and asked for the body of Jesus, and buried it.

My son, John: Remember what a loving and beloved disciple he was.

My daughter, Hope: Consider what a grace of God hope is, and covet after that hopes that will never be ashamed but has hope of eternal life and salvation of Jesus Christ.

My son, Obadiah: Consider that Obadiah was a servant of the Lord and tender in spirit, and in a troublesome time hid the prophets by fifty in a cave.

My son, Samuel: Remember Samuel was a chief prophet of the Lord, ready to hear his voice saying, "Speak, Lord, for thy servant heareth."

My daughter, Martha: Remember Martha, although she was encumbered with many things, yet she loved the Lord and was beloved of Him, for He loved Mary and Martha.

My daughter, Mary: Remember Mary who chose the better part that shall not be taken away and did hearken to the Lord's instructions.

My son, Jonathan: Remember how faithful and loving he was to David, that servant of the Lord.

My daughter, Lydia: Remember how Lydia's heart was opened, her care borne, her spirit made to be willing to receive and obey the apostle in what the Lord required, and was baptized, and entertained and refreshed the servants of the Lord.

"Be you content with your present condition and portion God has given you. Make a good use of what you have by making use of it for your comfort (solace). For meat, drink or apparel, it is the gift of God. Take care to live honestly, justly, quietly with love and peace among yourselves, your neighbors and, if possible, be at peace with all men.

"In what you can, do good to all men, especially to such as fear the Lord. Forget not to entertain strangers, according to your ability; if it be done in sincerity, it will be accepted, especially if to a disciple in the name of a disciple. Do to all men as you would have them do to you.

"If you would be Christ's disciples, you must know and consider that you must take up your cross and follow Him, through evil report and losses. But yet know, he that will lose his life for Him shall save it.

"Thus, my dear children, have I according to my measure, as is my duty, counseled you. May the good Lord give you understanding in all things and by His Holy Spirit convince, reprove and instruct and lead you into all truth as it is in Jesus. So that when you have done your work here, He may receive you to glory. Now the God of truth and peace be with you, unto Whom I commit this and you, even to Him be glory forever and ever, Amen."

ABRAHAM LINCOLN!

One of the reasons for including Obadiah Holmes in this book was to exhibit how a man, with a lineage of pastors, judges and college presidents such as the great Jonathan Edwards, can leave a legacy with his blessing, much like Jacob left his with Judah. One of Obadiah Holmes descendants was none other than Abraham Lincoln!

Old Honest Abe, claimed by the states of Kentucky, Indiana and of course, Illinois (the Land of Lincoln) was a direct descendant of Holmes's daughter Lydia! She moved to New Jersey and had a daughter named Sarah, who married Richard Salter. Salter's daughter Hannah married a man named Mordecai Lincoln.

Mordecai Lincoln's son was John Lincoln; called "Virginia John" His son was Captain Abraham Lincoln! He was killed by Indians in Kentucky in 1780. Captain Lincoln's son was Thomas Lincoln, the father of ABRAHAM LINCOLN – now called the greatest president of the United States of America.

Both Springfield's own Honest Abe and his grandfather were named Abraham. They came out of the legacy of Obadiah Holmes. Let's reread this part of Reverend Obadiah Holmes' last letter to his children, as he prepared to go home to Jesus. Here again is the part to Lydia Holmes. Lydia was the great, great, great, great grandmother of President Abraham Lincoln.

"My daughter, Lydia: Remember how Lydia's heart was opened, her care borne, her spirit made to be willing to receive and obey the apostle in what the Lord required, and was baptized, and entertained and refreshed the servants of the Lord."

Look at the love and Godly counsel passed on by this man of Christ – Obadiah – to his daughter Lydia. He recognized the commitment her daughter made to Christ, was baptized in the power of the Holy Spirit into the Kingdom of God. Lydia's descendants, through their pioneer spirit, led to the rail-splitter of Illinois.

From Obadiah to Abe Lincoln, the Legacy of Christ remained the thread. This does not mean everyone in this line were saved, justified, sanctified, glorified sons and daughters of Christ and are in heaven with him now. It does mean they had the opportunity to do so, along with coming from solid God-fearing American stock.

Other descendants of Obadiah Holmes include Baptist pastors and ministers down to this day! Some of his descendants on the Wightman side came down from Obadiah's granddaughter Susannah. She has been previously mentioned as the first wife of Rev. Valentine Wightman. The family grew and some settled across state lines in the great state of Connecticut, a state dear to my heart.

The Wightman Family moved from Montville, Connecticut to Herkimer County, New York. Later on, a descendant Benjamin fought in the American Revolutionary war for the Tryon Country Rangers of New York. The family grew in Herkimer County. Some of the Wightman line was also born in Kirtland, Lake County, Ohio. In 1835, one of Obadiah's descendants Charles Billings Wightman joined the Church of the Latter Day Saints – the Mormons.

He moved with his family in 1865. Traveling 2000 miles from New York by wagon into the Rocky Mountains, Charles settled in Payson. This was only 65 miles south of Salt Lake City, Utah . This is the line from which my new friend Ron Wightman descends. I am extremely grateful to Ron for supplying all this super family history from Edward the Martyr to Ron himself! There is so much rich American, Church and Family history in his story. This is Legacy; the legacy of three persecuted men of God – Edward Wightman, Obadiah Holmes and Roger Williams. To Him be the Glory and Honor and Praise, Amen.

All Wightmans are cousins of the Abraham Lincoln line! You can even say Ron Wightman is one of the last known 'kinfolk' of Honest Abe himself, even if Lincoln has no direct descendants!

4 Leadership 1.0

Outstanding people have one thing in common: an absolute sense of mission.

Zig Ziglar

"I thank my God, making mention of you always in my prayers, hearing of your love and faith which you have toward the Lord Jesus and toward all the saints, that the sharing of your faith may become effective by the acknowledgment of every good thing which is in you in Christ Jesus" (Philemon 4-6, NKJV).

What a victorious, encouraging verse by the Apostle Paul above to Philemon (a runaway slave)! Look at this key phrase: "the sharing of your faith may be come effective." What does Paul mean by "effective"?

The best definition of the word, which I found, is "productive; efficient; in operation; impressive or striking." If this is not the best definition of leadership, what is?

It is timely the word "effective" is used here. Look at this verse, in part, again: "BY THE ACKNOWLEDGMENT OF EVERY GOOD THING WHICH IS IN YOU IN JESUS CHRIST."

This means affirming, confessing and testifying to every benevolent and useful thing (agathos in the original Greek). To testify to something carries the connotation of Truth. Benevolence defines our Holy and Loving God who gives and gives from His bountiful Goodness! We testify to His benevolence or merciful kindness to us and admit He does this work IN US (reference the part of the verse that says "which is in you").

This entire phrase runs together ONLY on the foundation of the last three words of the verse:" IN CHRIST JESUS". We are nothing if we are NOT in Christ Jesus and He in us. If the reader does not have a personal relationship with Christ, I pray for you as you hold this book that the Spirit of the Living God works to draw you unto Him. This is the only way to experience the Joy we know so fully.

Therefore, having looked at this most instructive of verses, I wish to take a look at Effective Leadership, God's way! By the way, this verse was a prophetic word sent my way out of the blue just recently. Pastor Emeritus Donald Tabb is the man who started up the huge Chapel on the Campus of Louisiana State University thirty five years ago.

The former rodeo cowboy/US Army Ranger from Texas was once an advance pastor for Billy Graham's Crusades decades ago. One day, I was talking to him when he took was one word – effective – for him to pull out his King James and give me Philemon 6! God does speak through His Word!

In this unofficial handbook of Effective Christianity and leadership, we wish to examine four facets of Biblical leadership for the man or woman of God. Roles are clearly defined in the Bible and it is not the point of this dissertation to get into gender politics. What we will do is look at a few leaders in the Bible and see what made them great and then examine modern heroes of the faith and what makes them tick.

Four Facets of Leadership examined are: leadership in Evangelism and the church, in the Community, at work and home. To understand both men and women, we briefly touch on Stu Weber's Four Pillars of a man's heart and the Four Pillars of a woman's heart.

THE WARRIOR LEADER

There is an Arab proverb that says "an army of sheep led by a lion would defeat an army of lions led by a sheep." Exactly! Ultimately, we Christians are the sheep of our Shepherd, who is called the Lion of Judah!

As an army of sheep, we are ultimately led by the Commander in Chief and Shepherd in Chief, the Lord Jesus

Christ. However, He has ordained men and women on the earth to be His ambassadors in Jerusalem, Judea, and Samaria and even on to the ends of the earth. In modern terms, these could be Huntsville, Alabama; Lake Jackson, Texas and Brooklyn, New York or China, Calcutta or Cape Town, South Africa.

We can look at the four aforementioned Facets of Leadership in a vacuum as an academic exercise and close the book or we can look at the underlying qualities necessary to create that leader. First of all, we have to acknowledge leaders are generally not born. The old Vietnam hero Pastor Bobby Welsh was the most Evangelism-minded president of the Southern Baptist Convention ever. Dr. James Merritt is of course a hero of mine, but Bobby Welsh is cut from warrior cloth.

In his past tenure as president of the largest protestant denomination, he took Evangelism and the passion for souls to a 21st century passion. I would liken him almost to the great Dwight Lyman Moody. Moody stands head and shoulders above all as America's Pioneer Evangelist. Bobby Welch's nationwide bus tour of churches in the U.S. and Canada is in that genre.

Welch's book "The Warrior Leader" made a huge impression on me because it is the kind of man I want to be, even if I never had the knowledge and experience President Welch had as an evangelist and doer of the Word. He mentioned the U.S. Army (which he served so well) has three legs in its leadership foundation – Be, Know and Do.[18]

However, my leadership model for the Foot soldier of Christ (FSOC- my term) is fourfold – Be, Do, Know and Die! Why die in the Christ model but not the Army model? Good question! While a member of the U.S. Military should be prepared to die in combat or in the line of duty, the follower of Christ is expected to DIE TO SELF upfront.

---

[18] Bobby Welch, You the Warrior Leader, (Nashville, TN: Broadman & Holman Publishers, 2004), p. 2.

There are about fifty expectations which the Warrior Leader has in Bobby Welsh's book with a few of them listed here:

- Leaders don't run things, they lead
- Leaders have a vision that is clear bold and specific.
- Leaders have vivid imagination and bold FAITH.
- Leaders get people to reach levels they do not think possible.
- Leaders get people out of their comfort zone.
- Leaders let people get loose, puts the best people in the best opportunity.
- Leaders are not interested in running things but building people.
- Leaders are interested in everyone understanding and running with the vision.
- Leaders draw out workers' energy and creativity.
- Leaders often have team members who are brighter than themselves
- Leaders learn how to swallow their egos, lose their identities and expend themselves for others and the good of the vision.[19]

As leaders in our families, homes, churches women's or men's ministries, and community groups the first requirement is we know who we are. We should know ourselves as well as who we are in Christ Jesus. This is all about Him. I know many a ministry leader who has deluded himself because of whatever good works he/she is involved in, but there is no evidence of the Love of Christ in it.

Truth is more important than deeds. What good is it to have the best community outreach in the town or feed the most

---

[19] Ibid.

homeless or run the best rehab drug center if the Revelation 2:4 Test can not be passed? This is where Christ warns the church at Ephesus about all they are doing YET He found them lacking in Truth – they had left their First Love, Christ.

So the FSOC, the Warrior leader, has to know him/herself completely. Such a person needs to be the most humble and broken before the Lord DAY AFTER DAY or the entire exercise is academic. If the doctrine is wrong, the deeds are wood, hay and stubble.

What do the people who are led by the Warrior leader expect from him or her? Here again, Bobby Welch has many sought-after characteristics from the leader and only a few are listed below:

- The leader leads a Spirit-filled life.
- The leader lives by core values.
- The leader follows the correct motivation, mind, mission and ministry
- The leader leads by example.
- The leader is trustworthy.
- The leader admits mistakes.
- The leader has humility.
- The leader expands the army….to accomplish the Great Commission
- The leader plans and prepares.
- The leader challenges others and him/herself.[20]

As a grunt, a foot soldier most of my life, and a Warrior leader in other respects, I have been challenged to live all twenty something of the above items. The older and more mature one becomes in Christ, the easier it gets. However, it requires stamina, energy, commitment and a daily walk with the Lord.

---

[20] Ibid.

There is no better basic training for the ultimate Warrior leader than having your nose to the grindstone of truth. This is the best way to keep folks away from the proverbial millstone necklaces awaiting the unredeemed.

We have seen the expectations of a leader of him or herself and what the team expects of their leader, but what should a leader expect of his/her team? Here are a few last items on the Bobby Welsh list:

- They try to lead a Spirit-filled life.
- They are committed to learn.
- They are teachable.
- They live core values.
- They care for others.
- They are trustworthy.
- They too equip themselves to be Warrior leaders and live the attributes.
- They are humble.
- They have confidence and are decisive.
- They accomplish the Great Commission.[21]

All of this may sound a bit too militaristic for some folks. Even so, when Christ called us out to be in His Kingdom, He called us to a fight – the fight for souls and eternity. As we saw in previous chapters, He gave us the weapons – the Sword or the Good News of the Gospel.

Scripture did not say we should be in a kumbayah labyrinth of love of as we see in some of today's more liberal theology. The Bible says in Ephesians 6:12 NKJV "For we do not wrestle against flesh and blood, but against principalities, against powers, against the rulers of the darkness of this age against spiritual hosts of wickedness in the heavenly places." We are in a

---

[21] Ibid.

war whether we like it or not, and only the strong in Christ will survive unto Glory.

JOSHUA, ULTIMATE WARRIOR LEADER

When I asked Dr. Steve Farrar how he would sum up how he would describe the leadership style of God's own General, Joshua, Dr. Farrar had a simply powerful answer. He said "let the Lord go in front of you and fight your battles". Dr. Farrar is the men's ministry leader at the Chuck Swindoll's Stonebriar Community Church, Frisco, Texas. He is well known to Focus on the Family listeners and Promise Keepers Conferences during the 1990's.[22]

This is a most poignant description of the man's modus operandi; the same man who brought down the Walls of Jericho. Of all the millions who left Egypt led by Moses during the Exodus, Joshua and Caleb were the only two to make it into the Promised Land after 40 years in the desert. Both men where full of integrity, boldness and bravery. More importantly, they were obedient to the Lord and His commands.

- Joshua was a man of faith.
- Joshua was a man of courage.
- Joshua was a man of vision.
- Joshua was a man of loyalty.
- Joshua was a man of prayer.
- Joshua was a man of obedience.
- Joshua was a man of dedication to God.

HAVE THE FAITH OF JOSHUA

---

[22] All references to Dr. Steve Farrar and his materials are used by permission from Dr. Farrar.

We will briefly examine each one of these attributes and show what is expected of us as FSOC's –Foot Soldiers of Christ. Faith is the number one qualification. Moses had sent out twelve's spies to gauge the enemy in the land of Canaan. (Read the account in Numbers Chapters 13 and 14.) Ten came back whimpering. They said "sure the land is good and flowing with milk and honey BUT there are giants there…boo hoo (paraphrase!)"

Joshua and Caleb had a different spirit. These men of God remembered the promise Yahweh God made to Israel. Joshua's answer was "yep, there are giants – and we can take them"! Why? Read what Joshua said in from Numbers 14: 9-10 NIV: "Only do not rebel against the LORD. And do not be afraid of the people of the land, because we will swallow them up. Their protection is gone, but the LORD is with us. Do not be afraid of them. But the whole assembly talked about stoning them. Then the glory of the LORD appeared at the Tent of Meeting to all the Israelites."

Note Joshua said the giants could be beat. The Lord had removed their protection and the Lord was with them. This pure simple Faith in a Holy God by Joshua set him apart as the future leader of Israel. Sure the ungrateful former slaves of Egypt who were still slaves to their own sin wanted to stone the two Warriors of God, but the Lord Himself showed up in the Tent. Now when the Father shows up like this, it means trouble!!

All the characteristics of his faith give Joshua to both men and women as the ideal of faith. The giants we face today are enormous. They come at us with everything they have, straight from the pit of hell.

The giants are the judges of America who legislate their own morality. The giants are politicians who tell the unbelieving public anything they wish to hear. The giants are the media and Hollywood elite who feed our youth irresponsible pre-marital sex and drugs and rock 'n roll. The giants can even be found in the church where the Power of the Gospel has been replaced by the

PowerPoint of the feel good guru. But we who are sold out on Christ we can face them and take them out. Martin Luther said in "one little word shall fell him!" That word is Jesus.

HAVE THE COURAGE OF JOSHUA

Girded up by the truth of faith, we next need to have the same type of courage like Joshua. God told him in Joshua 1:7 "Only be strong and very courageous; be careful to do according to all the law which Moses My servant commanded you; do not turn from it to the right or to the left, so that you may have success wherever you go."

Strength and courage go together in leadership. Many times in the Book of Joshua, the Lord tells Joshua to be "strong and courageous." Remember what the mission was for him – go into a land of strange pagans, kill them and take it away! This was the Promised Land flowing with milk and honey.

So what is our mission? It remains the same! We are to go into a strange land, the highways and byways of our city and state, then America. To those whom God calls thus, they go into the ends of the earth. There will be no Second Coming of Christ until this occurs. I once saw a parody by one of my favorite people in the world, Ray Comfort. It describes the average church in America and their attitude towards Evangelism:

> Backward Christian soldiers, fleeing from the fight
> With the Cross of Jesus nearly out of sight.
> Christ our rightful master, stands against the foe
> But forward into battle, we are loathe to go.
>
> Like a might tortoise moves the Church of God
> Brothers we are treading where we've always trod.
> We are much divided, many bodies we
> having many doctrines, not much charity.

Crowns and thorns may perish, kingdoms rise and wane,
but the Church of Jesus hidden does remain.
Gates of Hell should never 'gains the Church prevail
we have Christ's own promise, but think that it will fail.

Sit here then ye people, join our useless throng
Blend with ours your voices in a feeble song
Blessings, ease and comfort, ask from Christ the King
With our modern thinking, we don't do a thing......
(Written by anonymous to the tune of "Onward Christian Soldiers")[23]

Now this can of military maneuver needs no courage! All one has to do is sit in the pew and think Evangelism is for those nuts on the street with the gospel tracts. Winston Churchill says "courage is going from failure to failure without losing enthusiasm." In Evangelism we will fail more times than win. I have been in many parades handing out Gospel tracts.

My favorite parade is the St. Patrick's Day parade in Springfield, Illinois. Our entire group is always decked out in Blood-red apparel to go with our 1955 American LaFrance fire engine affectionately known as ALF. Our fiery RED symbolizes the Blood of Christ and emblazoned on the truck is "ON FIRE FOR CHRIST".

It is amazing to see the eyes of people along the parade route as you attempt to hand them the good news on a tiny piece of paper, my friends!! You have never seen people recoil as they sometimes do. Another noticeable thing is the amount of dead eyes I have seen over the years looking back at me; eyes which do not know Christ at all. It is amazing the looks I get from all these bar patrons covered in Kelly green when a brown skinned

---

[23] http://www.livingwaters.com/articles_ray_archive/articles_ray_03-02-04_what battle.shtml*.

dude dressed in red shows up in front of their bar to hand them a gospel tract! That alone is priceless!

It takes courage sometimes to risk getting punched in the nose in front of those bars. But this is where the harvest is. It is not sitting in a church pew speaking to oneself saying "Lord, send revival" without first prayer and repentance, and secondly, Evangelism!

HAVE THE VISION OF JOSHUA

Thirdly, Leadership is Vision. We see Joshua's faith and courage. When you add vision, the uniform of the FSOC is starting to fill out. A visionary is one who has foresight and imagination. The foresight was provided by God. Joshua says "…. And do not be afraid of the people of the land, because we will swallow them up. Their protection is gone, but the LORD is with us. Do not be afraid of them…" Never mind the majority of Israel who now wanted to kill this "wacky optimist! Back to Dr. Farrar's definition of Joshua's leadership style – let God go before you and fight your battles.

Therefore, no leader in ministry, work, community or home can be successful without Christ preparing the way. Even in ministry, I have seen people with delusions of grandeur who appropriate the Lord's Name into every thing they plan, purchase or pontificate about, only to see the result as flat as a pancake! Be careful of this vision thing. It can only come from God. This happens in the office and at home as well. Every family has planned for different things with a goal in mind, only to see the Lord move in a different direction.

To the unredeemed, this is "bad luck". To those of us in the Will of Christ, God is saying "not so fast, bucko"! By the way, there is no such thing as luck. Luck implies chance and is associated with gambling. Nothing happens by chance. God is Sovereign and whether the world believes it or not, He is in control. So in order to have vision like Joshua, all we have to do is be still, know He is God and will make it clear. This type of discernment can only come from faithful prayer and fasting.

HAVE THE LOYALTY OF JOSHUA

Leaders are loyal, as well as faithful, courageous visionaries. At home parents are the leaders and we are loyal to our families to the nth degree. We are loyal to the United States of America. We are loyal to our favorite football team, the New York Jets!!!! Some Chicago Cubs fans..... (!!!) We are loyal to our employer or company. Are we this loyal to God?

There is no more act of Loyalty than Joshua's Farewell Address before he goes home to be with the Lord. Please read the entire chapters of Joshua 23 and 24. For this discussion, here are two verses from them. Joshua 24:14-15 NKJV says:

> "Now therefore, fear the LORD, serve Him in sincerity and in truth, and put away the gods which your fathers served on the other side of the River and in Egypt. Serve the LORD! And if it seems evil to you to serve the LORD, choose for yourselves this day whom you will serve, whether the gods which your fathers served that were on the other side of the River, or the gods of the Amorites, in whose land you dwell. But as for me and my house, we will serve the LORD."

The call is to serve God in sincerity and truth PUTTING AWAY THE GODS (which your fathers served). God knows if we are sincere or not. We are constantly tested to see if we are truly walking in the Light and if we fail, it is because we put the gods of this world before Him. These gods can appear to be good things as well as bad.

Modern gods are family, job, money, power, position, taking oaths to pagan gods in fraternal 'do-gooder' organizations etc. What? Family? Yes! If the Lord is not the Master of your house, someone else is! But "I do well at my job", is the cry. Unless we work as we would unto Christ, we are simply just working for a paycheck. This could take another book to develop on the other false gods of everyday life!

Suffice it to say things have not changed in 3400 years since Joshua. Human nature is still perverse and corrupt. No one seeks after God, not a single one. This is why the choice is now ours. We must decide, as leaders in one sphere or another, whom we are going to serve. The sooner this is settled, the better it would be!

Are we going to serve ourselves or our association with a select band of powerbrokers for the power base which some hunger? Are we going to be so base as to join some group of likeminded people which claim all gods are the same and then bow down to this universalistic false doctrine? Are we going to pour the world's values into our children and say all systems are okay, as long as you are sincere? OR are we going to recognize the One who caused us to be born in the first place and His intention was to have you become a worshipful child of His?

The choice is yours. One of the most famous verses in the Bible is Joshua 24:15 "AS FOR ME AND MY HOUSE, WE WILL SERVE THE LORD". This reads the same in almost every legitimate translation of the Bible. This is the true definition of Loyalty.

HAVE THE PRAYER LIFE OF JOSHUA

Prayer is the engine of our lives. Prayer is the spoke in our bike tire. Prayer is a symbol of our Love Relationship with our Creator. Be careful not to neglect it. There is a huge prayer in Joshua 7:2-15. I would like to focus just on a few verses. In part Joshua prays "Alas, Lord GOD, why have You brought this people over the Jordan at all—to deliver us into the hand of the Amorites, to destroy us?" (verse 7a, NKJV)

Now Joshua had just lost a battle at Ai (pronounced "eye") and the reason was the major sin of the Israel. God had turned His Holy Face away from them as certain of them committed abomination. The Lord demanded the "accursed" be removed physically and completely.

One thing to note here is we can not blame sin all the time for our defeats. In this instance though, and in others, it is obvious what brought disaster upon them – disobedience! For us, we need to seek the Lord for discernment and pray for wisdom. We can not heed the advice of Job's wife who told him to "curse God and die."

God said an interesting thing to Joshua which He has said to me recently, through my praying through a Scripture in a specific troubling situation. I have since shared this verse as prescient. The Lord said in verse 10, NKJV: "So the LORD said to Joshua: "Get up! Why do you lie thus on your face?"

I will never forget that Friday in February 2007. It was like a bucket of cold water right in the face! You have no idea how refreshing this verse is to me! GET UP OF YOUR FACE, AND QUIT WHINING is what I heard! It worked for me! It also worked for Joshua. He was one who believed all the promises of God, but at the first major defeat, he was whining about the entire rationale of the Exodus.

First of all, I feel more than blessed amongst men, the Lord will even speak to one such as I! It confirms the Lord speaks through His Word, and uses His Holy Spirit who lives within us to interpret the Word in us!

HAVE THE OBEDIENCE OF JOSHUA

Going back to Numbers 14: 10, we see "the congregation said to stone them with stones." The 'them' is Joshua and Caleb. Here is a 'congregation' willing to murder because someone dared to challenge their pessimistic view of God's promise! What this congregation did was to call God a liar! For that and other crimes against the Holy One of Israel, they would die in their sin in the desert.

Think about Dwight Lyman Moody. One person we all wish to meet in heaven is DL, as we Moody Bible Institute fans call him. We have all heard the story over our lifetimes about Moody being told he could not teach Sunday School. After all, who does this untrained, non-seminary schooled shoe salesman think he is? Well, DL had the answer for the conundrum.

He went out into the seamy streets of Chicago and convinced all the young boys to come to his own created Sunday School class. The very first week, he had 18 kids. He then first began teaching Sunday School to the unwanted children of Chicago on the shores of Lake Michigan! This led to his renting an old railroad boxcar as a classroom and an abandoned saloon. The drinking hall of sin and vice was converted to the Lord's use! From here Moody had such an impact; a former Windy city's mayor took notice. The ex-mayor donated an assembly hall. The rest was history!

D.L. refused to lay down in defeat. He was the ultimate prayer and preaching warrior of the 19th Century. He impacted the country from the 1850's up to this day. Here is a partial list of famous Moody Bible Institute (MBI) associates and graduates: Evangelist and prayer warrior R.A. Torrey; MBI Presidents Drs James Gray, George Sweeting and Joe Stowell. Alumni include authors Gary Chapman (Five Love Languages), Jerry B. Jenkins (Left Behind) and the great Baptist preacher/author Arthur W. Pink.

There are twenty one Moody Bible Institute alumni – men and women - who lost their lives in the cause of Christ, in countries at "the ends of the earth."[24]

---

[24] http://en.wikipedia.org/wiki/Moody_Bible_Institute

These "Stephens" walked in the obedience and were 'strong and courageous' as Joshua, God's General. They lived this verse from Joshua 23: 6-7 (NKJV):

> Therefore be very courageous to keep and to do all that is written in the Book of the Law of Moses, lest you turn aside from it to the right hand or to the left and lest you go among these nations, these who remain among you. You shall not make mention of the name of their gods, nor cause anyone to swear by them; you shall not serve them nor bow down to them.

Joshua warned the Twelve Tribes over and over in both Joshua Chapters 23 and 24 during his Farewell address. What we need to take away from this most stunning address is the consequences of disobedience as a people. Not only had God rescued them from slavery in Egypt but He wiped out completely huge pagan nations to give the Land flowing with milk and honey to His people, Israel.

The battle was not easy. The burden on Joshua and his army was tremendous as they led ungrateful, sometimes disobedient people into Canaan. God has done the same for this blessed country, America. In fact NO other country in western civilization has been so blessed by Almighty God. He seems to have a special place for America because of the Godly Principles of its founding. Just look at the lives of people like D. L. Moody and see the obedience of the Great Commission.

HAVE THE DEDICATION OF JOSHUA

The man God chose as His General was as single focused, as any leader should be. That object of his complete focus was the Holy One of Israel. It was the Lord who brought Joshua through battle after battle.

It was the Lord who kept working on his behalf. It was the Lord who told him "be strong and courageous and do not be afraid". Through it all; through every bloody battle; through the miracles of the sun standing still for a day; through the miracle of the flooded Jordan River rolling back like a scroll; God was there for Joshua. How much more then would He be for you?

The encouragement is to be like Joshua and "take diligent heed to yourselves to love the Lord your God" (Joshua 23:11).

A great example of dedication to the Lord is Anna the prophetess. Now she was not prophesying like Isaiah or Jeremiah. Here is all the Bible says about her in Luke 2:36-38 (NIV): "There was also a prophetess, Anna, the daughter of Phanuel, of the tribe of Asher. She was very old; she had lived with her husband seven years after her marriage, and then was a widow until she was eighty-four. She never left the temple but worshiped night and day, fasting and praying. Coming up to them at that very moment, she gave thanks to God and spoke about the child to all who were looking forward to the redemption of Jerusalem"

If there was a picture of Dedication to the Lord, it was Anna. Note a major point here – "she never left the temple". My life verse of Scripture is Psalm 27:4 KJV (One thing have I desired of the LORD, that will I seek after; that I may dwell in the house of the LORD all the days of my life, to behold the beauty of the LORD, and to enquire in His temple). The New American Standard Bible translates the underlined phrase literally as "meditate in His Temple."

The Hebrew translation would apply to Anna in her mission in life – she continually sought the Presence of the Lord through the protection and security in His Temple. She found all that through prayer and fasting. She worshiped day and night. This is so powerful. Even in my own little time of a fraction of this kind of worship, the Revelation of the Lord is so powerful. Can you just imagine Anna's dedication?

God the Father rewarded her faithfulness and dedication in worship with wisdom. Because of the intimacy with the Heart of God to one who fasts and prays, Anna could do things in this male dominant culture, most men could not do! This was also a culture where women were relegated to second class status. So what did Anna do?

This statement is very powerful and revealing: "Coming up to them at that very moment, she gave thanks to God and spoke about the child to all who were looking forward to the redemption of Jerusalem." God gave her the unique and tremendous privilege of not only meeting the infant Jesus, but to prophesy and speak about Him to the assembled.

This is huge. Luke tells the Bible reader a. Anna may have been the only woman to "preach" in the Temple and b. it was the first official presentation of Baby Jesus to those in the Temple who were eagerly awaiting the Messiah.

What awaits the dedicated man or woman of the Lord is Jesus! The One True Pearl of Great is His Name Price (among the other 177 Names of Christ).

What awaits the dedicated leader is Divine Revelation. What awaits the dedicated leader is wisdom and discernment.

The woman or man God chooses to be His leader, in whatever capacity, needs to have all these seven attributes of Joshua. I can think of no better example of a completely Effective leader…right out of God's Word!

He was fearless from the beginning. Sure there are giants, but we can take them! He was obedient and faithful to the end. As he headed of to the bosom of Abraham, Joshua threw down the gauntlet to those he had led into the Promised Land of milk and honey.

It was now up to them to stay true to Holy God. The Bible actually affirms they did remain faithful….at least those who came into the land with Joshua. This is the legacy of a strong leader. He not only inspired them to follow the Book of the Law, but to live it as he did. The fact they took him up on it for a time is a testimony to the power of his witness.

The next chapter briefly examines the Four Pillars of both a man's and woman's hearts as well as how we lead in four key aspects of life - family, church, community and work.

5 Leadership 2.0

"Too bad that all the people who really know how to run the country are busy driving taxi cabs and cutting hair"……
George Burns

The Good Lord has given us His model for Biblical Leadership – His General Joshua. How we apply it to various facets of life take experience and understanding roles. Over the past decade many books and seminars have been written to get both men and women to step up to various forms of leadership in all spheres of life.

The past two decades have seen all kinds of movement's crop up which attempt to provide the basis for leadership in the home and the community for both men and women. Iron John was a book written in 1990 by author Robert Bly which decried the lack of masculine men, male mentors and the male spirit.

I remember the stories of guys going out in the woods to bang drums and discover their inner warrior self in the wilds of nature. The Promise Keeper (PK) movement began on more than a fast clip and soon had millions packing Football stadiums around America as well as the Washington D.C. Mall for Stand in the Gap. It has been responsible for at least 90% of men's ministries in the Churches of America. (The Seven Promises of the Promise Keepers are seen below and there are timeless values, whether for men's or any other type of ministry!)

1. Honoring Jesus Christ through worship, prayer and obedience to God's word in the power of the Holy Spirit.
2. Pursuing vital relationships with a few other men, understanding that he needs brothers to help him keep his promises.
3. Practicing spiritual, moral, ethical and sexual purity

4. Building strong marriages and families through love, protection and biblical values
5. Supporting his church by honoring and praying for his pastor and by giving his time and resources.
6. Reaching beyond any racial and denominational barriers to demonstrate the power of biblical unity
7. Influencing his world, being obedient to the great commandment (see Mark 12:30-31), and the great commission (see Matthew 28:19-20).[25]

    Then the Men's Fraternity movement came out of Fellowship Bible Church in Little Rock, Arkansas. Developed by Dr. Robert Lewis in this once small church, Men's Fraternity has gone where PK left off. Dr. Lewis attracted a lot of non-believers to his early morning classes in Little Rock where over 1000 men would show up to his weekly leadership training classes.

    What attracted them as well as our believing brothers was Dr. Lewis using the Word of God to pierce the darkness of men's heart and teach them how to live in victory. Several were saved and reconciled to families. Hundreds more discovered their hidden father or mother wound and vowed to not repeat these with their own kids.

    Even more were set on a path for the Great Adventure – the Life abundantly promised by God for His people. A lot of us were already at peace with our God, but were not maximizing the gifts He gave us for His Glory. Men's Fraternity has now gone international, impacting men and families for Christ and continues to help a growing number of men, from all backgrounds and ages, develop their God given gifts.

    Again we go back to the biblical definition of a leader – faith, humility, faithfulness, obedience, faithfulness….and did I

---

[25] www.promisekeepers.org.

mention faithfulness? Divorce amongst Evangelicals is rampant and just as bad as the secular world.

One of my heroes is Dr. Al Mohler, the dynamic and fearless leader of Southern Baptist Theological Seminary in Louisville, Kentucky. On June 11, 2006 he had eye surgery. He then showed up on June 12, on the first day of the 2006 Southern Baptist Convention in Greensboro, N.C. to debate another seminary president on election of the saints with his eyes bandaged up so he could not see his notes! He did not need his notes. A man of Christ needs only the Holy Spirit as his eyes!

His daily blog, of June 9 2007, mentioned the waning credibility of us Evangelicals on marriage, as if we live in a parallel universe to the rest of the world. This is not good. We have the best God has given us in the abstinence movements. Let us be resolved to drum this into our children who are brainwashed daily into a sexualized culture while the church remains silent.

Some churches and youth group leaders, who really gave a hoot, have rediscovered the True Love Waits program (and similar ones). Cervical cancer is now afflicting so many teenage girls (of no faith as well as professing Christians), that now is the time to teach purity and abstinence. Why do I say "give a hoot"? Well, a lot of modern mega churches and their wannabee clones are single focused on experimenting with too many modern fads in music, worship and style and are minimizing the basics. Gone are the true biblical disciplines of discipleship, outreach and service.

FOUR PILLARS OF A MAN'S HEART

One of the most unique books I ever attempted to read was "Men are like Waffles, Women like Spaghetti" by Bill and Pam Farrel Harvest House Publishers, 2001. The entire premise of their book was understanding and enjoying the differences between men and women. The Farrels correctly say men are like those little boxes on waffles; namely men compartmentalize and can only do or focus on one thing at a time! They say women are like a strand of spaghetti wound all over the dish, as they multitask holding the baby while talking on the phone and kicking the door shut with their feet!

All of this is true. I readily acknowledge I am no expert on this kind of thing. Therefore, I take comfort in the Bible and am careful about what I know, less I fall. To get to the point of how a leader operates in community, work, church and home, we have to understand the individual.

Before we move on, one thing comes to mind. From biology days, we know the heart has Four Chambers. The two upper chambers are called the Atria. It is here the blood flows into and NOWHERE else. The lower two chambers are called the Ventricles. It is from here the blood leaves the heart and NOWHERE else I accentuated these because each level of chamber has its function which follows form. It works no other way.

One of the most famous works in the Christian Living book revival of the past 25 years is Stu Weber's "Four Pillars of a Man's Heart: Bringing Strength into Balance". In it, Weber presents a case for what every boy wants to grow up to be; what every man needs to develop in himself and even what every woman may want in a husband.

Weber uses the Bible as a basis for the model of the Four Pillars of a Man's Heart. You can almost see Weber the imagery of the Four Chambers of the Human heart here! I will list each point and give a brief commentary.[26]

Pillar Number one is the Heart of a King! Here the man follows Biblical examples like Abraham, Isaac and Jacob by offering justice and mercy to others. So much so that even our family may think we are nicer to other people than to them. This is not necessarily correct but showing mercy at the Mission or

---

[26] Stu Weber, <u>Four Pillars of a Man's Heart : Bring Strength into Balance</u> (Sisters, Oregon: Multnomah, 1993), p. 13.

other acts of community services brings out the True Leader in you. The Heart of a King is the noblest of all.

Pillar Number two is the Heart of a Warrior. I know of no man in my circle of Christian brothers, even co-workers, who would not lay down their lives for his loved ones. Jesus said in John 15:13 "Greater love hath no one that he would lay down his life for his friends". He was talking about Himself while giving us the example of the kind of leader we need to model – Him! My best friend is my wife, Vicki. I would do the same for her, or our kids.

We already examined the Warrior Leader and namely the Ultimate Warrior leader – Joshua. Well, men are called to be just like him, in order to be Christ like. Christ is the Prince of Peace. God is Love. This is all true! Look at what Jesus said: "Do not think that I came to bring peace on the earth; I did not come to bring peace, but a sword". When He comes in Judgment, He will be swinging more than a cord of whips at moneychangers.

The entire Bible is full of military imagery. Paul did not tell us to put on the Velvet Vest of God, but the FULL ARMOR. We are in a war. We are in a war for the Kingdom, for our families and our freedom. Do not fall for the false idols of an increasingly Godless Western society which has diminished the role of the Biblical male. Evangelical Christianity is the last bastion of true manhood. Both pillars – the heart of a king extending Grace like King Jesus, and the Warrior heart must work in sync to defend this Fortress of masculine freedom.

Pillar Number three is the Heart of a Mentor. This is the chamber of a man's heart which leads him to want to pass on a legacy. In an earlier chapter we saw an amazing story of two ordinary preachers from Salem, Massachusetts. Obadiah Holmes and Roger Williams were two mavericks who refused to along with Infant Baptism man-made traditions of the Puritans (who got it from the Church of England and the Roman Catholics). For that they were tried as heretics and later banished.

After both men set up shop in Rhode Island, they became the foundation of the huge Baptist church of America. Generation after generation of pastors and preachers did not just happen. These men and their descendants poured their lives and the Word of God into their children who passed it along.

No one takes the time anymore to be a mentor and this is worse in the church, where it should be happening. For instance now I have an older, wiser brother in Christ Gene Grman who has taken an interest in making sure I have the correct biblical view of theology for most of the past few years I have known him. Before that, there was another 80 year old now-deceased brother in church who literally groomed me to become a teacher of prophesy starting with the Book of Zechariah.

However, I have since found out, I am blessed amongst men in this regard. Not many people I know (who are not pastors) have a godly elderly mentor. Of course, many may have a wise brother or sister of his/her age group they can call on for counsel. American Christianity is to blame. Legacy and discipleship is not preached anywhere. Therefore the leader whom God raises up needs to find him/herself around Godly men and women who would pass on their wisdom or be mentors to them.

Pillar Number Four is The Heart of a Friend. This defines the part of a man who is compassionate and loving. In the Bible we can think of best friends such as David and Jonathan or Paul and Timothy. What occurred between Paul and his former protégé John Mark really spoke to me at this point in the book. Here is a good lesson to learn on how to reconcile with a friend.

John Mark was not a disciple. It appears he was present at Jesus' arrest by the Temple soldiers in the Garden of Gethsemane. Mark 14:51-52 carries a noteworthy account of a man who escaped the arresting soldiers, running away naked when they grabbed the linen sheet he had around him! Most Bible scholars take this to be Mark himself, when he was just one of Jesus' followers. Later on, during the second stop of Paul and Barnabas' first Missionary Journey, guess who ran off again –

this time to Jerusalem! He was taken on by Paul because he was one of the Lord's followers and his running off during serious evangelism did not sit well with the Apostle.

The next time they were preparing for another Evangelistic outreach or journey, Barnabas requested Mark be taken along with them. Paul, formerly Saul of Tarsus, said "absolutely not"! This caused a split in the Evangelistic team (read the account in Acts 13) as Paul took Silas and Barnabas went off on his own outreach with Mark.

Barnabas was a mentor to Mark as the elder of the two and shepherded him along the fierce paths of preaching in the Nazarene's Name. He encouraged him patiently and watched the growth. Being part of the same family also meant a lot to this relationship.

John Mark committed two errors in his life as a follower of Christ. He ran when Judas betrayed the King. So did His Disciples. He turned and ran back home to Jerusalem when his cousin Barnabas and Paul hit possibly a harsh new town to spread the gospel. So do we when the giant calls out our name.

Mark's restoration to Fellowship was complete. The Lord forgives youthful fears and actions, all the time….and He still does!! AMEN!! Paul heard of his elevation in the Eyes of the Lord and was so impressed that years after wanting nothing more to do with John Mark, he asked for Mark to come join him in 2 Timothy 4:9-12. This was near the end of his life as he awaited execution to go home to Jesus.

This same John Mark wrote the Gospel of Mark! It is only appropriate the half brother of Jesus – James – would write the first book of the New Testament. HOWEVER the very first Gospel ever written was by this young lion of the Faith – John Mark. It is the most easily comprehended of all Four Gems.

What does this have to do with the heart of a friend? Everything! In spite of all the inter-ministry friction between two Giants of the Faith – He who is a Friend of us all, and calls us friend, can do greater things with weak and wounded sinners we can ever imagine. It is quite possible Paul was preaching out of Mark's Gospel in his later years for background flavor. Mark learnt a lot of his Gospel from talking directly with Simon Peter.

The Four Chambers of the Human heart and the Four Pillars of the Spiritual heart are almost seamless. Just as in the human heart, the top two in-flow chambers receive life-giving blood from the lungs etc, the Spiritual heart's top two pillars (of a King and Warrior) receive their commission from the Giver of Life.

Just as the lower two ventricles of the Human Heart pump the blood received from the upper chambers out, the last two pillars of the Spiritual heart (of a mentor and friend) are meant to be used for Kingdom work. I take this to mean that the Power and Love we get from Christ and every part of the Holy Spirit is meant to be poured out of us into those around us in the world. To do anything else would make us bloated on our own self-righteousness and fat in our own favor.

LEADERSHIP IN THE COMMUNITY

The voluminous work of the past more than a chapter and a half gets us to the point where we take who we are as men and women of Christ, into the community at large. For Christians to have an impact on the people around us, we must have the following:

- A product to sell (The Good News).
- A plan to accomplish it.
- A process to implement
- A plan B if plan A fails
- A people to lead.
- A Perfect God to Praise when the plan succeeds!

Most leaders are not born, they are made. Moses was a fugitive from Egyptian justice. Gideon was a coward from a family who worshiped idols. King David was a shepherd boy with a gift from God and the gift of God. Peter was a hot headed fisherman. All these Biblical heroes had one thing in common – Passion! They threw every fiber of their being into the Service of the Holy One of Israel.

I do not know if you are like me and love old Bible movies. There is one about King David and one scene in particular which had such an impact on me, I want to live it. (This movie has Jeff Chandler in the role of King David and was made in 1960.) Read the following narrative from 2 Samuel 23: 13-17 NIV.

> During harvest time, three of the thirty chief men came down to David at the cave of Adullam, while a band of Philistines was encamped in the Valley of Rephaim. At that time David was in the stronghold, and the Philistine garrison was at Bethlehem. David longed for water and said, "Oh, that someone would get me a drink of water from the well near the gate of Bethlehem!" So the three mighty men broke through the Philistine lines, drew water from the well near the gate of Bethlehem and carried it back to David. **But he refused to drink it; instead, he poured it out before the LORD.** "Far be it from me, O LORD, to do this!" he said. "Is it not the blood of men who went at the risk of their lives?" **And David would not drink it.** Such were the exploits of the three mighty men. (Emphasis mine)

Look again at the bold phrase **"and David would not drink it"**!! The movie reenactment of this was more powerful than reading it. Here was the man who wrote in the Psalms about a dry, thirsty land. Yet he poured out the only water he and his warriors had as a Drink Offering to a Holy God. This was even more powerful than the widow's mite in the New Testament.

The question we need to answer from the deepest part of our being is, are we ready to pour ourselves out in the Service of the Lord like King David? Sometimes leadership in community service calls for just this kind of sacrifice. I have seen it in men who run the Christian Homeless missions in Springfield. I have seen it in minister to the Homeless Scott Payne, who is a close brother and a member of our Men's Ministry – Business Men in Christ. It is not easy, yet it is a testimony to your mission and Mission, when you turn away 500 people in one year, because your Inner City Mission is full to capacity.

From leading and participating in regular Bible studies at the IC Mission over the years, I have noticed the spiritual progression of certain folks, whom the world had turned its back on. All of this happened because men like Scott Payne, his wife and family and a committed Christian staff 'poured out the water to the Lord'. Am I saying secular homeless missions, especially those who take money with governmental strings attached are not capable of life-altering Transformations like the ones we witness at Inner City Mission?

Yes! There is nothing; no psychotherapy; no Darwin/Freud psychobabble teaching comparable to the Liberating Truth of the Gospel of Christ. A good exercise would be to invite the enemies of Christ and His Evangelical church to name the great missionaries and mission homes around the world OTHER than those run by North American Evangelical Christians! Despite all the money Arab sheiks make off selling oil to the West, how do their people live? Southern Baptist Franklin Graham's Samaritan's Purse can be even be found in Muslim countries providing food and medicine. Name its counterpart?!!!

There is no need to expound on the points laid out earlier on Community Leadership. However as we follow these points to effect solid Christian service in our communities, we do need to be aware of the pitfalls and how to deal with conflict.

Of the abovementioned steps, the most complicated is not the plan but the people who are being led. Everyone comes to the table with different gifts, backgrounds, values and principles. We must never assume everyone in Christian ministry or work is a saved, sanctified son or daughter of the Living God. Wait until you see the fruit.

The Effective Leader must prepare for conflict before it even happens and know the way out of it. When it comes do not avoid it, slight it or gloss over it. Deal with it head on. As usual, the Bible shows the way for competent leaders to handle situations.

Matthew 16:15-17 NKJV says "Moreover if your brother sins against you, go and tell him his fault between you and him alone. If he hears you, you have gained your brother. But if he will not hear, take with you one or two more, that 'by the mouth of two or three witnesses every word may be established.' And if he refuses to hear them, tell it to the church. But if he refuses even to hear the church, let him be to you like a heathen and a tax collector".

This is the model from Christ for Church discipline as well as para-church organizations. The key is to do it in love, even if it is tough love. Jesus' guidelines in this passage are full of love. He gives the sinner many chances before the latter is to be cut loose from the team.

LEADERSHIP IN THE CHURCH

The same principle of conflict resolution works inside the church as it does in the real Harvest field for the church. The requirements for leadership for Christ's church however are very different and more defined. There is a big reason for this. Pastors/ teachers, elders and deacons are more accountable for their stewardship than anyone else. "Obey your leaders and submit to them, for they keep watch over your souls as those who will give an account. Let them do this with joy and not with grief, for this would be unprofitable for you" (Hebrews 13:17). The church is supposed to represent Christ on earth. If the church has no influence in moving its immediate sphere of influence its leaders are going to have to account for everything they did. I was a deacon for almost three years. When I thought I could be more effective elsewhere – i.e. in the leadership of Business Men in Christ – I resigned.

QUALIFICATIONS OF AN ELDER, BISHOP, DEACON

The reason for including the following long passage from 1 Timothy 3: 1-15 AMP is to show the qualifications for Church leadership. If anyone reading this book feels called to this aspect of ministry, fill up with the measure of your call against these Scriptures to see if you are found wanting or affirmed.

THE SAYING is true and irrefutable: If any man [eagerly] seeks the office of bishop (superintendent, overseer), he desires an excellent task (work). Now a bishop (superintendent, overseer) must give no grounds for accusation but must be above reproach, the husband of one wife, circumspect and temperate and self-controlled; [he must be] sensible and well behaved and dignified and lead an orderly (disciplined) life; [he must be] hospitable [showing love for and being a friend to the believers, especially strangers or foreigners, and be] a capable and qualified teacher, not given to wine, not combative but gentle and considerate, not quarrelsome but forbearing and peaceable, and not a lover of money [insatiable for wealth and ready to obtain it by questionable means]. He must rule his own household well, keeping his children under control, with true dignity, commanding their respect in every way and keeping them respectful. For if a man does not know how to rule his own household how is he to take care of the church of God?

He must not be a new convert, or he may [develop a beclouded and stupid state of mind] as the result of pride [be blinded by conceit, and] fall into the condemnation that the devil [once] did.

Furthermore, he must have a good reputation and be well thought of by those outside [the church], lest he become involved in slander and incur reproach and fall into the devil's trap. In like manner the deacons [must be] worthy of respect, not shifty and double-talkers but sincere in what they say, not given too much wine, not greedy for base gain [craving wealth and resorting to ignoble and dishonest methods of getting it]. They must possess the mystic secret of the faith [Christian truth as hidden from ungodly men] with a clear conscience. And let them also be tried and investigated and proved first; then, if they turn out to be above reproach, let them serve [as deacons]. [The] women likewise must be worthy of respect and serious, not gossipers, but temperate and self-controlled, [thoroughly] trustworthy in all things. Let deacons be the husbands of but one wife, and let them manage [their] children and their own households well. For those who perform well as deacons acquire a good standing for themselves and also gain much confidence and freedom and boldness in the faith which is [founded on and centers] in Christ Jesus. Although I hope to come to you before long, I am writing these instructions to you so that, If I am detained, you may know how people ought to conduct themselves in the household of God, which is the church of the living God, the pillar and stay (the prop and support) of the Truth.

My friends, do not take this lightly. There is going to be many a pastor, elder or deacon not in Heaven when the roll is called up yonder. They were not His in the first place. Others will be held accountable for missed opportunities; financial mismanagement and not listening to the people sent by the Holy Spirit.

1 Peter 4:17 gives a dire warning and please take it seriously. Peter says "For the time has come for judgment to begin at the house of God; and if it begins with us first, what will be the end of those who do not obey the gospel of God?"

Judgment Day will begin with Christ's people first and it will be decided if all the works of the church will burn up like wood, hay or stubble. Do not believe the lie of soft modern American Christianity. This is leading countless thousands into the Lake of Fire with weak theology and lack of teaching of the repentance of sin. Do not be weighed in the scales and found wanting.

Finally, do not be a non-praying church. Almost every church in America is a non-praying church. I do not mean a pastoral prayer during the service or prayer requests during Sunday school. I am talking a continued consecration and calling out to Christ to come and concentrate His Spirit in the presence of His Bride to the Glory of His Name. This can only come about through repentance and renunciation of our sins as a corporate body. The evangelical church in America is not a praying church. Why? Because we think we have nothing for which to repent!

LEADERSHIP IN THE HOME

I can add nothing to what the Bible says about Biblical leadership in the home for parents. Various ministries have cornered the market on this from Dennis Rainey's Family Life to Ken Canfield's Fatherhood Ministry. But Christ is always teaching me something I can never read in any books or learn at a seminar about being a father and conversely Vicki, about being a mother.

DANGER ZONE

The job of parents is to raise our children to be God-fearing adults who are their own person, yet remain completely dependent on Jesus. This is the biggest job we will ever have, not the one with the Tuesday deadline at the office. That job can pass as we are disposable employees. As Christ's own, however, no one can snatch us out of His Hands.

There are several more criteria which can be added but here are some of the responsibilities we have as parent leaders. I got them no particular place. The following list is a collection of my wife's and my experiences learnt the hard way over the preceding years. On behalf of our children, we are:

- To lead them to a saving knowledge of Jesus Christ as their Savior and the way to eternal life.
- To lead them to excellence in education based on Absolute Truth and Christian values.
- To lead them to critical thinking on their own.
- To lead them to empower and enhance their own lives through that kind of thinking.
- To lead them to the realization that because of their standing in Christ, they have unlimited opportunity.
- To lead them to realize this is America and the sky is the limit.
- To set their eyes on several goals and ways to accomplish them
- To set their minds on the possibility of failure and how to deal with it.
- To set their eyes upon Jesus and all will be well, in failure and success.
- To set their hearts on Prayer and to do nothing without it.
- To learn to respect authority, especially when authority or they are wrong.
- To learn those in authority are more responsible to God, both believer and non-believer.

- To learn while those in authority may be unfair and discriminate against you, they are still more answerable to a Holy God than you are.
- To learn life is not fair, so get on with it.
- To learn from their parents' principles so they can pass them on to their children.
- To learn the attributes of the Warrior from the previous chapter as well as those of God's General Joshua.
- To learn to apply these attributes to everyday life in all aspects of adolescence and then adulthood.
- To learn purity in thought, word and deed in a morally perverse and corrupt world where even those placed in authority are more concerned with their ideology than your eternal welfare.
- To learn from young, the value of a dollar and moderation in everything.
- To learn from lean times how to manage limited resources, since they would not live in comfort and ease starting out as an adult or newlywed down the road.
- To learn healthy habits as the wages of the physical sins of lust, fornication, alcohol, tobacco and even misuse of firearms are DEATH.
- To learn to accept the Godly guidance of their parents so they can avoid going to secular, no-nothing, Freudian-influenced therapists when they get older.
- To learn to look to the Bible which has the answer to every single problem known to mankind?
- To learn there are no excuses on Judgment day before God. He will judge according to Truth, Deeds and what the Gospel says.
- To learn God will judge both action and attitude, so be careful of their attitude to both the ministry and Christ's ministers, even if some are hypocrites.
- To perform random acts of kindness.

- To perform Godly sacrificial service to the less-privileged among us.
- To develop a heart for service.
- To develop a mind of steel, welded unto the Gospel of Christ.
- To develop the mind God gave to live in Truth – don't lie, your lie would find you out.
- To develop the propensity and pray to God for Courage to defend the Truth – as many will denigrate and try to deceive them as life goes on.
- To develop the strength, through Christ to stand for the Truth, so they will never fall for the Lie.

LEADERSHIP AT WORK

The majority of people are not in management and this could be a good thing! Uneasy is the head that wears the crown and ultimately - very uneasy if the crowned head is without Christ. But did you know we can be leaders at work in our own little way.

We assume this mantle from Kingdom authority. We who are called by His name carry His authority with us. We are not responsible for creating the organizational plan. However, we are responsible for executing it. He is responsible for its success. We, who have His Spirit, are empowered by THAT authority over what He has given us and therefore can claim it in certain situations.

So how can we use this opportunity as a worker, even those of us at the lowest rung in the ladder, to bring Glory to God?

Well, we build off the same attributes of Joshua, the Ultimate Warrior. Those Biblical principles never change. These are the foundational truths. Where we work is a positional truth, FOR A TIME.

Our salvation and standing with Christ is NOT positional. It is eternal. Who we are is NOT defined by what we do to help pay the bills. This is the domain of small minded non-believers in a wealthy, materialistic society on their way to eternal Judgment. Who we are is defined by our Faith and Trust in Jesus Christ and Him alone, as Lord of our lives.

The job we work in, at the present time, was provided by God. This is true whether we believe it, or not. Therefore do your job as you would, unto God. This truth is for the majority of us in the fields, as well as those in a supervisory capacity over us.

Read the following narrative from Genesis 2:15-17 NKJV "Then the LORD God took the man (Adam) and put him in the Garden of Eden to tend and keep it. And the LORD God commanded the man, saying, "Of every tree of the garden you may freely eat; but of the tree of the knowledge of good and evil you shall not eat, for in the day that you eat of it you shall surely die."

The first sentence above was the first work assignment in human history. God prepared the way and gave Adam simple instructions. Adam chose to disobey and blame. Since the Resurrection of Christ and our standing as His Hands and Feet, by HIS choice, we have several duties to fulfill before He moves us, promotes us, or allows us to be dismissed. The following list comes out of years of walking with Christ among folks who profess a belief or none in Jesus. In the workplace we are:

- To conduct ourselves with open integrity and character without reproach.
- To care for the soul of even the most unpleasant nonbeliever in the office, shop or factory.
- To condemn blasphemy among our work colleagues and not fellowship with unrepentant sinners, who refuse to refrain from such conduct.
- To correct what is not right about God and Christ with your co-workers, in a loving way.

DANGER ZONE

- To carry His Name and the Truth of the Gospel to these same people.
- To speak up when He directs you.
- To silence yourself when He is about to do the work Himself to either convert someone His way, or mark them for destruction on Judgment Day, by their own conduct.
- To use every opportunity to reflect the Work of Christ in our lives.
- To use every opportunity to pray for your colleagues and share the Gospel in a way relevant to the situation.
- To use every opportunity to minister in every imaginable way, as the Spirit directs, to make a small difference in someone else's family's life.
- To refrain from inappropriate jokes and using profanity at all times.
- To refrain from sexual and other inappropriate comment about women at all times in all situations.
- To refuse to go along with others to bars and other after-working hours establishments to "celebrate" birthdays or other events. Such events compromise your witness and mark you as a hypocrite.
- To refuse to go to lunch with any member of the opposite sex alone.
- To not become involved in the personal problems of any member of the opposite sex, unless they ask you for pray for them.
- To not become involved in any man-made fraternal or any organization which DOES NOT have Christ at the center of its entire being.
- To minister to brothers in Christ (if you are a man) or sisters in Christ (if you are a woman) and encourage them to soar to greater heights in the Lord, as a result of you being there for them at all times. This strengthens our

Testimony and we are fulfilling one mission of Christ – to show how easy His yoke is and how light His burden is.

To do these things prayerfully, day after day, takes maturity and discipline. The key is to become mature in the Ways of God through constant daily study and immersion in the Word of God. It is spiritually profitable to listen to only uplifting Gospel and Christian music of all varieties.

Modern technology makes this so easy in these last days, one can find Christian radio stations or videos and CDs everywhere from Wal-mart to your secular video store. Sky Angel is a much better choice of Television for the family than anything HBO or MTV could ever devise from the pit of hell.

We should fellowship constantly with fellow believers when in hostile environments. Remember we are the shrinking remnant of His people on this earth. Those of us who are stronger and more fearless for the Cause of Christ are responsible for those who are under assault by the forces of this world, and can not react. We are to pray for, cheer them up, supply them with resources and encourage as much as possible.

Marketplace Evangelism is the most effective of all. Sunday church is mainly for the flock. Dr. Adrian Rogers once said "we gather for worship; we scatter for witness". Jesus hardly spoke to large crowds. The Gospels record few instances of the Lord speaking to outdoor mega-churches and then He was Pastor/Teacher. It was deemed as few as to warrant prominence in the Gospels. All the major lessons Jesus taught for our benefit, were presented to either one person face to face or the small group of hypocrites (or Pharisees).

His Word ALWAYS pierced their very souls! When He called Matthew, the latter was Levi the corrupt tax collector as was Zaccheus. We have more opportunity to be salt and light in a tasteless, dark, dying world than the average Preacher in the pulpit. Let's git 'er done!

6 Fourth and Goal

"For I am already being poured out as a drink offering, and the time of my departure is at hand. I have fought the good fight, I have finished the race, I have kept the faith. Finally, there is laid up for me the crown of righteousness, which the Lord, the righteous Judge, will give to me on that Day, and not to me only but also to all who have loved His appearing."
2 Timothy 4: 6-8 (NKJV)

The majority of working Americans, including some Christians, spend almost all of the entire second half of their working lives counting down to retirement. Why? A lot of them, including some with whom I work, just can not wait to stop working – so they can do nothing! Many new retirees who build their financial nest eggs and obsess about them in their forties and fifties basically place them all in a proverbial basket. This basket puts complete human faith in a concept of life without the Sovereignty of God. Even our own Evangelicals forget who is in charge and map their lives out according to human plans.

Here is what the Lord said in Luke 12:19-21 (NKJV) "And I will say to my soul, "Soul, you have many goods laid up for many years; take your ease; eat, drink, and be merry."' But God said to him, 'Fool! This night your soul will be required of you; then whose will those things be which you have provided?' "So is he who lays up treasure for himself, and is not rich toward God"

Believers are never meant to spend the Fourth quarter of life playing golf, driving around in RV's, restoring classic cars and making them mini-gods or living the life of Riley on stock dividends. Each day is a gift of God to be cherished. Each breath is a grant from the Father. Each moment of life is Grace from above. Never assume He owes us anything except eternal punishment for our rebellion.

Were it not for the Savior's death on the Cross, we would be receiving our just rewards of eternal damnation. The above verses are Truth and should not be taken lightly. There is no allegory here, but literal fact! The poet Robert Burns said in his Poem (To a Mouse) – "the best laid plans of mice and men often go awry".

Christians are not supposed to look forward to another season of life as the world does. We know better. Our God placed us on this planet for His Service, His Pleasure, and His own purposes. It does not matter if you are a Calvinist or an Arminian or an in-between (belief in some free will), but accepting most of the TULIP of Calvinism. One thing is sure - He who made the Heavens knew us before the Foundation of the World.

TULIP is the acronym for "the Total Depravity of man, Unconditional election, Limited Atonement, Irresistible Grace and Perseverance of the Saints. The TULIP is the backbone of Calvinism.

This is not an endorsement of Calvinism. Like a lot of other literal Bible students, I have trouble with the Calvinist belief of Limited Atonement – meaning Christ only died for the elect. The Cross was for all, for all time. What this means is He set a path for us. Whether we choose to obey Him and stay on that path is totally up to us. We will all stand before the Judgment Seat of Christ one day, where He will test our works by fire for rewards. What we did with our time will determine our reward in Heaven.

The late Dr. Jerry Falwell was the head of Liberty University, Lynchburg, Virginia which is one of the finest of any educational colleges in America. Many years ago, he came up with some points about Fourth Quarter Christians in ministry and life.[27] We do not have to go back to Abraham, Joshua and Caleb and the Patriarchs of the Faith to see examples of men or women

---

[27] Dr. Jerry Falwell's Fourth Quarter Ministry: Thomas Road Baptist Church. http://sermons.trbc.org/21100805.html.

who 'died with their' boots on or changed the world in their latter years!

Think of Ronald Reagan who became president of the United States at age seventy! His story is well known, except for the fact he was very private about being a born-again Christian. Is there any other kind? Think of the late Sir Winston Churchill who was called back to save Great Britain during World War II at age sixty-five. Reagan won the Cold War against the evil Soviet communist empire and Churchill set the standard for generations of world leaders in the free world. Churchill was not a believer as we see in his dying hopeless words. However the man had tremendous wisdom.

So how should one approach the game in the Fourth Quarter? The main points (in bold) are from Dr. Falwell, to which I added my own commentary. They give us some guidelines whether we are in ministry in a church or a volunteer at a nursing home.

1. **You live life looking forward, but you understand life looking backward.**

In other words, you can not know where you are going until you know where you came from. When Christ saved you and me, He brought us out of the Egypt of our own sin.

He had already passed over our own door posts by dying on the Cross. He parted the Red Sea to get us onto dry, safe land. But He took us through the desert. He took us through thirst. He took us through rebellion as at the waters of Meribah. He took us through bickering and disappointment. Because of the Cross, we get to cross the Jordan with Him into the Promised Land!

We can not comprehend the Promised Land until we understand the Wilderness of Zin. We can not appreciate Heaven and Paradise, until we remember Egypt. We can not appreciate Grace until we look at the Law and see the vile nature of our forgiven, repented sin!

2. Your success in the Fourth Quarter begins long before the game begins.

This makes absolute sense. Whatever we plant, we sow. How many times have we watched a football game and seen the team leading with the score at halftime, sit down and try to run out the clock. Unfortunately, this describes a lot of Christians, even some of our more solidly mature ones! We all know the stories of 5% of folks in the churches, doing 100% of the work, while the other 95% wait to be served.

Do not sit on the lead! Do not run out the clock! How many times we have seen a team running out the clock, make a mistake, turn the ball over on downs and end up losing. If we lose the game in the Fourth Quarter, the Coach will not be too happy.

Coach Jesus called and gave us the correct play. He provided the strategic blocking for OFF TACKLE RIGHT which works every time He calls it. Why on earth would His people begin killing the clock right after half time? The audible calls we make on the line, changing the play on the fly after thinking we read the changing defense, will have impact more than we can ever know! Disobedience is a heck of a misread!

3. The greatest thing about the fourth quarter is still being in the game.

Following on point number 2, even if we are disobedient and change the play on the line from the one Coach Jesus sent in, He gives us 2nd and 3rd down to move the ball. There has never been and will never be another Coach like ours. He is the Alpha and the Omega and there is none like Him. He can yank us from the field. Many have been benched for rank disobedience because He will not allow His children to sully His Name. The fact is He allows us to be hit in the backfield, get up and run straight up the middle again right behind the center. Jesus is not into long bombs and Hail Mary's!! He is definitely not into Hailing Mary! He is methodical and sticks to the playbook. He was born of a virgin, but existed before she ever did.

4. The longer you stay in the game, the more comfortable you get playing the game.

Those of us who became believers and Warriors late in our lives wished we had done this, years ago, when we were in our teens! The problem is we were not mature enough back then to even notice we were in need of a Suffering Savior. We needed to go through the Valley of the Shadow of Death, die to our sins and be redeemed by the Blood of the Lamb.

Psalm 23 says in Verse 4 (KJV) says "yea though I walk through the Valley of the Shadow of Death, I shall fear no evil…" We fear no evil because a Shadow can not hurt us! Jesus defeated death on the Cross! King David was living in victory (Psalm 110: 1, KJV…"the LORD said to my Lord, Sit Thou at My Right Hand, while I make Thine enemies a footstool!).

Yet he got so comfortable in the Lord, he broke all the Commandments in the Bathsheba incident, repented in Psalm 51 and was restored. Then he fumbled the ball again when he pridefully took a Census, against the specific instructions of God and his people were punished by the LORD in a severe famine. Again David was restored! The lesson to learn here is thus – do not get so comfortable in what we think we are doing FOR God that we fail to protect the ball with both arms wrapped around it, and try to carry it with one arm. The enemy's linebackers are cunning and evil enough to go for the knees and knock the ball loose! Hold on to Jesus! Do not fumble; we are in the Red Zone!

5. Even though the game gets more comfortable in the fourth quarter, it never gets any easier.

Many things in ministry seem easier to deal with as time goes by due to the fact of Christ's power dwelling or abiding in us. Abiding is a sweet word. The original Greek word is MENO and among its meaning is "to continue to be present". It is a present tense. Roget's Thesaurus gives a number of words we can use to expand on the true meaning of "abiding". They are: establish oneself, hole up, hang out, live at, lodge, occupy, reside, room, stay and tarry! I like the first phrase "establish oneself".

Once we are established in Christ Jesus and live in His Word, it does get easier to fellowship with Him. It is more comfortable being in the heat of battle on the field. No matter what the opposing side throws at us, we can rest in the Knowledge of the Holy. Psalm 119:32 (NIV) puts it succinctly: "I run in the path of your commands, for you have set my heart free."

Now this is good news BUT NEVER sit on a lead, as we discussed earlier! Our enemy, the Devil, roams the earth like a roaring lion seeking to devour whomever he can. He takes extreme pleasure in bringing down God's people who allow the power of sin to cloud their new nature in Christ. The deeper to the Red Zone with First and Goal; it is hard enough to score. We also lose yardage by willfully sinning and giving up yardage to the devil.

6. I'm a better team player in the fourth quarter.

This is very true! Age does not equal maturity. I have seen younger men who live more in Sabbath rest, in Him, than men who are older by 20 or 30 years.

First of all, we acquit ourselves by the very manner and attitude by which we perform these necessary duties. I speak from experience from one who still cleans church bathrooms with my family for the past 12 years. When one is faithful in little things, one is then entrusted with weightier matters. Furthermore the Body of Christ has already been designed thus, as in Ephesians 4:

11, 12 (AMP): "And His gifts were [varied; He Himself appointed and gave men to us] some to be apostles (special messengers), some prophets (inspired preachers and expounders), some evangelists (preachers of the Gospel, traveling missionaries), some pastors (shepherds of His flock) and teachers. His intention was the perfecting and the full equipping of the saints (His consecrated people), [that they should do] the work of ministering toward building up Christ's body (the church)."

7. **The longer you stay in the game, the better perspective you have of the big picture.**

In the game of Life, one does not expect a rookie to start the first game of the season. The more experienced quarterback always gets the call because he knows the plays, can read the defense and can audible to change the play on a dime.

One does not expect Broadway Joe Namath of the New York Jets to fall for a stunt by a Baltimore Colts linebacker in Super Bowl III when he was reading almost every counterattack as if it were written in large print. So it is with the Christian. Once I came off the bleachers and was sent in with a play called by Coach Jesus, I was on a horizontal playing field. This meant both my peripheral and distance vision were equally horizontal. But the plan He has laid out involves vertical line of sight! We must look upward to get the only accurate big picture there is. Likewise, our vision is perfect like Namath.

Too many Christians think and play horizontally. The Cross is made up of two pieces of wood: one horizontal and the other vertical. Christ's arms are open wide in the horizontal position. His Head and Heart are pointed north into Heaven. Never lose sight of the Heart of Christ as we move ahead on the ground. Both directions together give us the correct perspective on why we are even in the game!

8. In the fourth quarter, you're not as distraught about your past failures.

It is said "if at first you don't succeed, think of how many people you made happy!!" We believers chuckle at this but have a different point of view on our past failures. What the world calls a failure, Christ uses as a training tool! I like the verse from Job 13:15a "though He slays me, I will hope in Him!" This is the ticket.

This is the way to look at the Lord's molding us into a people called out for His work. Hebrews 12: 6 says "those whom the Lord loves, He scourges." Look however at verse 11 which says "All discipline for the moment seems not to be joyful, but sorrowful; yet to those who have been training, afterwards it yields the peaceful fruit of righteousness." The many failures in my own life were my own fault. They came about because I was not walking with the Lord or was disobedient. But the merciful Lord He is, He brought me through it! The Breakthrough He provided was more that I ever deserved! It is worth repeating; when He tests are with fire, DO NOT ignore!

Playing in the best part of the game – the Fourth Quarter – allows us the wisdom to recognize when the Lord is in something we consider fierce or unfair. This is when Satan's demons work in the lives of the mostly non-believing people we work with or for in our secular jobs. How we respond to these satanic attacks, even if they bring failure, exhibits the level of our spiritual maturity.

9. In the fourth quarter, you return to your tried and proven methods

In the section on Leadership, we looked at some proven methods from the best of the best. I am talking about men like Bobby Welch who applied several proven military leadership to

Evangelism methods. The Christian world is full of all kinds of "new" and "exciting" other ways to reach the lost.

It is amazing the sizable percentage of the mainly "mega churches" (relative to city size) who have shucked their old members, gone millions into debt and gone totally into the post-modern marketing model of church philosophy. In the process, some of them lost some of their older members who are opposed to these massive seeker-sensitive structures.

It is also amazing the lengths certain ministry leaders think they have to go to appeal to their favorite demographic – the young and restless! In all this, I fail to see the relevance to the Reverence towards the Holy One of the Universe. I am sorry, but I am not a fan of the modern ways emerging out of the darkness.

The fear of many of us forward looking evangelists, who are grounded in the solid hymns of the faith and traditional faith, is these seeker-sensitive based churches are creating a number of converts who were not regenerated by conviction of their sins! Our fear is they are swayed by nice sounding music, drama, dance and tickling of the ears by non-offensive preaching from the paraphrased versions of the Bible! The Tried and Proven methods are still the only way, whether it is the Fourth Quarter or the opening kickoff. There is a reason Ray Comfort (www.livingwaters.com) and Kirk Cameron are exploding all over Christian TV with the Way of the Master weekly program. The only way to bring the Good News of the Gospel is the way Christ did and Charles Spurgeon preached – use the Law to show the need for a sinner. There is no sugar coating this!!

10. The greatest thing about the fourth quarter is the confidence you develop.

Some of the great college football teams from my favorite Alabama Crimson Tide to the black and blue Big Ten Division teams like Michigan and the Illinois Fighting Illini always stress the fundamentals. The great Bear Bryant of the Tide was a stickler for the book but also bucked the system. It is well known among football fans what Bear did to bring black football players into the Tide back in 1971. He was strong enough as the Bama coach to integrate the Tide when then Democratic Governor George Wallace was in full reign against the Civil Rights movement. Bear's confidence came from a non-nonsense modus operandi his entire life.

It is not an accident his attitude led to his preaching fundamentals on the field – discipline and the fundamentals. Roll Tide! With the proper foundation, any one in the game will be confident of his or her place in Christ.

We have seen it in organizations, sports teams and the like, the more the fundamentals are executed with precision, the more confident they become.

11. In the Fourth Quarter you learn how to play with pain!

We serve a Suffering Savior. The entire chapter of Isaiah 53 is about the Suffering Servant of Almighty God the Father. He, who had no place to lay His Head, was beaten so much He was beyond recognition. One of the many objections to Mel Gibson's Passion of the Christ was its bloodiness. But in a major sense, that was one of the most accurate things about the movie. The world, including some weak-kneed Christians, did not want to face up the bloodguilt it has by what was done to Jesus Christ.

The whips laced with metallic scraps which tore into His flesh were graphic and historically accurate. The Lord's face was unrecognizable. By the way, this makes the famed Shroud of Turin a major hoax. So how do we play with pain?

Most avid football fans remember the Miami Dolphins – San Diego Chargers Monday Night Football game in Miami back in 1981. It is a game which makes highlight reels for the great Tight End of the Chargers, Kellen Winslow. Winslow was dehydrated and suffering numerous injuries. That game has stuck in my memory for the past 25 years for its sheer magnificence of a man who gave it all on the field.

Not only did he block a field goal, in his pain, but had 13 receptions for 166 yards and 1 touchdown – an NFL record at the time. He had a pinched nerve, severe cramps that rendered him almost immobile as he walked in slow motion, a cut lip with 3 stitches and dehydration. The memory of two teammates almost dragging him off the field at the end of the game which the Chargers won 41-38 is an NFL classic replayed over and over again.

We are not Kellen Winslow. However when the devil knocks us down; blindsides us; hit us below the belt; chop blocks our knees; clotheslines our necks or gives us an illegal contact upside our Helmet of Salvation, we get up; praise the Lord; take a swig of Living Water and get right back in the game!

This game of Life which Christ calls us to is not for the weak. When He saves us He not only puts us on the field but expects us to put on the uniform He provides for us. Ephesians 6 gives us a full description of the Armor of God. Too many of our fellow travelers go out in the marketplace of ideas without their Armor. They subsequently get beat up, defeated and then turn away from the fight or in some cases, from the faith completely. The latter were never saved in the first place.

Just as a football team has specialized positions for each man, so Jesus has provided gifts and talents to His men and women who are called by His Name.

Dr. Robert Lewis has a phrase in his public church ministry Men's Fraternity, The Great Adventure, where he teaches "function follows form." In other words, you can not take a duck and try to train it to fly like an eagle. A duck is a duck. A church pianist should strive to be the best she or he can be. The friendly usher/greeter has a special function in the church and so on.

Not everyone is called to be a pastor, and believe me, not everyone who is a pastor was called either! The regular church member in the pew can be more of an evangelist than the entire church staff put together. She or he has the opportunity to reach more worldly doubters at the office or the marketplace and witness by their words and deeds. Sometimes one can try to reason too much and appeal to the intellect with people who are steeped in Darwinism and their own self-righteousness.

This is the case with me at times in my encounter with the secular world weekly. So how the Lord has gotten around this, is to have me fellowship with a very small select group of fired up believers known only to ourselves at work! He has His Own way of training you for His Work here on earth.

MID LIFE CRISIS

One can not speak of Fourth Quarter Christians without addressing what is a classic North American phenomenon – the Mid Life Crisis! Countless men, wiser and more educated than I, have addressed this in seminars, books and other teaching tools. I do not seek to be like them! I come from a conservative Christian Caribbean background. This thing about men in their forties or fifties suddenly ditching their beautiful wives of their youth to buff up in the gym then go driving a red corvette accompanied by a 20 year old blonde bimbo, is totally anathema to me….and to Christ!

No man or woman of God should to succumb to this secular pattern of misbehavior. Do not buy all this garbage you see advertised in these lurid magazines and tabloids at the check out line in the supermarket. These things such as Cosmopolitan and Redbook give such much filthy advice to women; it can only come from the pit of hell! These so-called self-help magazines and their book counterparts sell the lie of a "guilt-free" fantasy life "as long as you do no act it out". This is another lie from the master of lies, Satan.

Why buy counsel from some columnist in New York City who sits behind a word processor transferring his or her own twisted thoughts to print while stopping in a bar on the way home to drown whatever their demons are? Beware this so-called Fantasy life. Jesus warns in Matthew 5:28 (AMP) "But I say to you that everyone who so much as looks at a woman with evil desire for her has already committed adultery with her in his heart." This applies to both men and women.

One's thought life is the first thing which should be guarded from the evil one. The great Zig Ziglar, appearing on the Focus on the Family radio broadcast many years ago gave the best application to guard your heart from straying. He prays every morning for the Lord to build a Wall of Fire around his heart, so NOTHING can penetrate it – no harlot, no temptation, and no compromising situation. I have since taken his advice.

The minute one allows a thought to take hold; it leads to situations I have seen numerous times in my past 35 years of work, to the destruction of families.

Here is what pop psychology tells you about a Mid Life Crisis. Jean Coleman, MSC, a consultant clinical psychologist says "mid life crisis is characterized by low mood, dissatisfaction with life, a feeling of pointlessness in life. It is not always distinguishable from clinical depression."[28]

She also says those in crisis may show their distress by reacting in several different ways: "by denial (by escape or overcompensation), by decompensation (with anxiety, depression or rage), or by regression. An individual may become discontented at work, resort to alcohol or risk taking behavior.

The range of feelings experienced have been variously described as hollowness and lack of genuine enjoyment, emptiness and uncertainty, a mixture of strain and boredom, floating unfocussed melancholy and depression. This is the time when people are believed to be vulnerable to hypochondria, accidents, illness, alcoholism and suicide.

---

[28] Jean Coleman, the Society for the Study of Androgen Deficiency, London, England. http://www.andropause.org.uk/Articles/aboutus.asp.

Midlife crisis is described as an existential crisis, that is to say, it is centered about issues of meaning and purpose in life. This is why it arises at the time it does, because by the mid thirties, young people have often achieved their initial goals in life or realized they are not attainable"

AHA!! There it is! EXISTENTIALIST CRISIS! To understand the modern North American version of Midlife Crisis, one has to delve into what Existentialism really means and how American society has become so totally wrapped up in this humanistic philosophy.

The best description I can find is from Dr. Bob Corbett, Professor Emeritus of Webster University of St. Louis, Missouri. Dr. Corbett is a very nice man and has since retired to his garden, gourmet meals and watching European Soccer!! From all he said, life is good even with a six month stint on a Federal Grand Jury in Missouri! He gave me permission to us this very classic and textbook explanation of the characteristics an Existentialist, to wit:

- They are obsessed with how to live one's life and believe that philosophical and psychological inquiry can help.
- They believe there are certain questions that everyone must deal with (if they are to take human life seriously), and that these are special -- existential -- questions. Questions such as death, the meaning of human existence, the place of God in human existence, the meaning of value, interpersonal relationship, the place of self-reflective conscious knowledge of one's self in existing. Note that the existentialists on this characterization don't pay much attention to "social" questions such as the politics of life and what "social" responsibility the society or state has. They focus almost exclusively on the individual.
- By and large Existentialists believe that life is very difficult and that it doesn't have an "objective" or

universally known value, but that the individual must create value by affirming it and living it, not by talking about it.
- Existential choices and values are primarily demonstrated in ACT not in words.
- Given that one is focusing on individual existence and the "existential" struggles (that is, in making decisions that are meaningful in everyday life), they often find that literary characterizations rather than more abstract philosophical thinking are the best ways to elucidate existential struggles.
- They tend to take freedom of the will, the human power to do or not do, as absolutely obvious. Now and again there are arguments for free will in Existentialist literature, but even in these arguments, one gets the distinct sense that the arguments are not for themselves, but for "outsiders." Inside the movement, free will is axiomatic, it is intuitively obvious, it is the backdrop of all else that goes on.[29]

In high school, one of my literature books was "The Stranger" by Albert Camus. This book messed up my mind for years because I was not a regenerated, Holy Ghost- saved, sanctified believer. I was a 16 year old pup who had written the US Navy the year before so I could join and go fight in Vietnam! I thought there was some kind of glory in getting anonymously shot down on the battlefield!

However it said a lot about my philosophy – namely, I had none!! I went to church, youth group, missions, etc…but I was Camus' Stranger on the beach. Camus is one of the leading Existentialists of the 20th Century. I did not know until now he

---

[29] Bob Corbett, "What is Existentialism" March 1985.
http//www.websteruniv.edu/~corbetre/philosophy (Used by Permission).

was an atheist! So were all the others like Franz Kafka or Jean-Paul Sartre.

So the Midlife Crisis' roots ARE existential and totally wrapped up in self, devoid of God. The Christian who is living by the Life of Another (a favorite phrase of my friend, the great Bob Warren, Bible teacher and former San Antonio Spur) is NOT an existentialist.

The Christian exists to please Christ and walk in His Light. How many times do we hear in the latest fad book, talk show, song, TV show....basically the secular American culture, the following, in no particular order nor author, just from observations over 30 years:

- You are free! So love yourself. Be yourself. Do what you wish. You are not hurting anyone!
- Think big! Think outside the box! You better think!
- You deserve that car! Charge that coat! Take that cruise, pay later! Just charge!
- Live like there is no tomorrow! Grab all you can now! Tomorrow never comes!
- The choice is yours! "Go on try it, you'll like it!"
- "She won't know, you are only looking!"
- "Oh I love him....and I don't care if he is married with four kids...."

This love of self is what is placing a cancer in American evangelicalism and causing some otherwise rational Christian men to fall. Needless to say, even the strongest among us must take heed, lest we fall. For goodness sake though, why participate is this New Age sacrament? A person, male or female, whose life is so full of prayer and is totally sold out to Christ, would seek to do NOTHING which would hurt the Heart of God. When we were saved by Him, we took on His Nature. Our old Adamic Nature was disposed with. Let us act like the saints we have become.

DANGER ZONE

The following verses from Romans 6: 1-13 (AMP) are so rich and relevant to any Christian's life that they must be quoted fully and in context. Like it did Martin Luther over 500 years ago, these verses in Romans opened my eyes permanently with a peace which passeth all understanding! These verses are the only way to glorious living, living by the Life of Another, and living in Victory.

> WHAT SHALL we say [to all this]? Are we to remain in sin in order that God's grace (favor and mercy) may multiply and overflow? Certainly not! How can we who died to sin live in it any longer? Are you ignorant of the fact that all of us who have been baptized into Christ Jesus were baptized into His death? We were buried therefore with Him by the baptism into death, so that just as Christ was raised from the dead by the glorious [power] of the Father, so we too might [habitually] live and behave in newness of life. For if we have become one with Him by sharing a death like His, we shall also be [one with Him in sharing] His resurrection [by a new life lived for God]. We know that our old (unrenewed) self was nailed to the cross with Him in order that [our] body [which is the instrument] of sin might be made ineffective and inactive for evil, that we might no longer be the slaves of sin. For when a man dies, he is freed (loosed, delivered) from [the power of] sin [among men]. Now if we have died with Christ, we believe that we shall also live with Him, Because we know that Christ (the Anointed One), being once raised from the dead, will never die again; death no longer has power over Him. For by the death He died, He died to sin [ending His relation to it] once for all; and the life that He lives, He is living to God [in unbroken fellowship with Him]. Even so consider yourselves also dead to sin and your relation to it broken, but alive to God [living in unbroken

fellowship with Him] in Christ Jesus. Let not sin therefore rule as king in your mortal (short-lived, perishable) bodies, to make you yield to its cravings and be subject to its lusts and evil passions. Do not continue offering or yielding your bodily members [and faculties] to sin as instruments (tools) of wickedness. But offer and yield yourselves to God as though you have been raised from the dead to [perpetual] life, and your bodily members [and]faculties] to God, presenting them as implements of righteousness.

Our sins can be anything from coveting a friend's new Mercedes to looking more than once at temptation as she passes by. Let us consider ourselves "dead to those sins", live in peace, joy and contentment in Christ and watch any so called Mid-life Crisis become just another man-made theory. In other words picture yourself like Paul in Philippians 4:11 "Not that I speak from want, for I have learned to be content in whatever circumstances I am."

HOW THEN SHALL WE LIVE IN THE FOURTH QUARTER?

If there was one man in the Bible who lived a permanent Midlife Crisis it was King Solomon! His prayer at the dedication of the Temple when he chose Wisdom over riches one of the most beautiful, heartfelt prayers in the entire Scripture is still the standard for believers. I used this prayer to pray the Lord for wisdom, His wisdom, more than anything else in my own life.

However from then on for old King Solomon, it went downhill. The wonderful love of his life in the Song of Solomon has become the benchmark for couples Bible studies nationwide. From the Song of Solomon, he went to Proverbs 21:9 "It is better to live in a corner of a roof than in a house shared with a contentious woman." He went from the Love of his life to his

DANGER ZONE

700 wives and 300 concubines (1 Kings 11: 1-3)! He came full circle in the final quarter of his life when he repented and wrote the book of Ecclesiastes.

Chapter 11 of this book gives us wonderful direction on life. The entire chapter is a joy but the key verses in my opinion are verse 1-2 (NIV): "Cast your bread upon the waters, for after many days you will find it again. Give portions to seven, yes to eight, for you do not know what disaster may come upon the land."

The original Hebrew translation of these verses is "Send your substance [out] over the face of the water [i.e., the sea] that you may find it [again] many days hence. Give a share to seven, or even to eight, for you cannot know what [sort of] disaster may come upon the land." This is even richer than the English translation! Ecclesiastes 11 (NIV):

> Cast your bread on the surface of the waters, for you will find it after many days. Divide your portion to seven, or even to eight, for you do not know what misfortune may occur on the earth. If the clouds are full, they pour out rain upon the earth; and whether a tree falls toward the south or toward the north, wherever the tree falls, there it lies. He who watches the wind will not sow and he who looks at the clouds will not reap. Just as you do not know the path of the wind and how bones are formed in the womb of the pregnant woman, so you do not know the activity of God who makes all things. Sow your seed in the morning and do not be idle in the evening, for you do not know whether morning or evening sowing will succeed, or whether both of them alike will be good. The light is pleasant, and it is good for the eyes to see the sun. Indeed, if a man should live many years, let him rejoice in them all, and let him remember the days of darkness, for they will be many. Everything that is to come will be futility. Rejoice, young man, during your childhood, and

let your heart be pleasant during the days of young manhood. And follow the impulses of your heart and the desires of your eyes yet know that God will bring you to judgment for all these things. So, remove grief and anger from your heart and put away pain from your body, because childhood and the prime of life are fleeting.

Solomon was the wealthiest man in the world and had diversified into all kinds of products which made him the envy of the known world! But his uncontrollable lust led him to worship the pagan gods of his many pagan wives. He set the table for the utter devastation, decline into depravity and death of the nation Israel!

His legacy was a split Kingdom with his sons and their descendants becoming some of the vilest enemies of the Living God. So when he repented and wrote Ecclesiastes, we need to listen to him, who was once a man after God's own heart.

So what does "Cast your bread" mean?" First of all, we must be bold. Boldness runs throughout the rest of the chapter. By being bold and not afraid to take risks, we are encouraged to invest wisely. One invests wisely in seven or eight different ways to avoid putting all one's eggs in one basket. He is using metaphors not just for financial prosperity but in any aspect of life.

Some Bible teachers also point out the larger meaning of verses 1 and 2 to the mature Christian. I can not remember where I heard the following but it reveals a lot of truth. For instance, Middle Eastern bread is light and can float on water for a while. By this random act, one is almost doing what some say: "do good, throw your bread out in the water, if the fish does not know it, God does!" I take this to mean when one constantly thinks of others in the context of investing time, resources and the Love of Christ in them without expecting a return, one is less likely to obsess in the worldly standard of "SELF" above all else. Hence verses 1 and 2 of Chapter 11 carry a double meaning which is so rich and poignant.

The rest of the verses are full of life changing truths to support the poor and be generous. He encourages us not to wait for the weather to change but to do today whatever we can do. A person whose life is hidden in Christ, Colossians 3:4 (Christ is my life), will be joyful (verse 7) and enjoy life by thanking Him for each new day.

Solomon warns in verse 9 not to be become dazzled by the things of the world, supposedly as he did. Finally in verse 10 he admonishes the reader to make the most of our years, as youth and life is so fleeting.

Chuck Swindoll summarizes the entire chapter rather well in one of his many sermons on the radio: "Start activating your life today and never quit…Refuse to let your life collect dust. Start today. If you don't start today, chances are good you never will. Don't wait for the weather to change. Don't wait for the kids to grow up. Don't wait for your husband to come back or your wife to return. Don't wait until you have spare time or more money or stronger health or a better job or a bigger house. Don't wait for conditions to be perfect. Be bullish about this, starting today. And never quit,"[30]

One can almost see Swindoll flashing the big smile of his as he expounds this truth!

The mature Christian who has been in the game for all four quarters and lived Ecclesiastes 11 can look forward to walking off the field when the whistle blows and the Roll is called up Yonder to a crown of glory for a life well –lived.

As Solomon says, there is 100% unemployment in the grave, so let's get to work now and seize the day!

---

[30] Chuck Swindoll's "Insight for Living" Radio Broadcast, Plano, Texas.

7 Christ in the Zone

He has showed you, O man, what is good.
And what does the LORD require of you?
To act justly and to love mercy
and to walk humbly with your God.

Micah 6:8, NIV

MEN IN THE AMERICAN EXPERIENCE

American manhood has always been defined in terms of rugged individualism. It is a mindset burnt into the fabric of American life from the can-do days of men like President Theodore Roosevelt who epitomizes American Ascendancy in the world. As the 20th Century became America's century, more and more, American manhood began to be redefined in a number of ways – some of which God has never ordained.

In a sign of the coming Culture of Celebrity, Hollywood described a real he-man as someone with the onscreen exploits of silent screen actor Rudolph Valentino or the kick- down- the-door rough and tumbling John Wayne.

The first half of the century gave us men's men and what some called Christian men like General Douglas MacArthur, General George Patton, and General Dwight D. Eisenhower.

Actually, of all the men named above, only General MacArthur made more than one huge public profession for the Lord. The good General was both a man's man and God's man!!

According to the Public Broadcasting Service (PBS) series on the American Experience called "MACARTHUR", the General's biggest disappointment was not being able to convert the entire island of Japan to Christianity! He said "true democracy can exist only on a spiritual foundation," and will "endure when it rests firmly on the Christian conception of the individual and society."[31]

If a U.S. General talked like that today in this era of anti-Christian bigotry and universalism, they would call for his head on a platter! In the same PBS TV documentary, he also said this about the Philippines "A Christian nation, the Philippines stand as a mighty bulwark of Christianity in the Far East, and its capacity for high moral leadership in Asia is unlimited."[32]

There are many examples of speeches made by MacArthur where he shared testimony to the Lordship of Jesus Christ.

America was defined by many events in the first half of the 20th Century. These ranged from the Glory Days of Teddy Roosevelt to World War 1; from the Roaring 20's and its lawlessness to the Great Depression and on to World War II.

Each time period gave us men who stood out and, even today, are cited as the epitome of American manhood.

None of us could ever forget Saturday afternoon westerns with the great Audie Murphy, the most decorated soldier of World War II. Audie joined the United States Army in 1942 at the age of 18. He was only 5 foot 5 inches tall and weighed 110 lbs! But he managed to kill 240 German soldiers and received this country's highest honors.

John Wayne was not an actual Military hero, but had the profile of patriotism and passion for the American way of life. His movies are not only favorites of aging fifty year olds like me, but our children as well. They spelled American, where our ideals are "Good will always triumphs over Evil."

Wayne believed in American exceptionalism and even wrote a book called "America, why I love her"! He reigned

---

[31] Public Broadcasting Service, The American Experience "People and Events – MacArthur, WGBH-TV, Boston, MA, (1999).
[32] Ibid.

supreme as the example of American manhood until the 1970's when Mr. Cool took his place! Clint Eastwood hit the consciousness of America like a lightning bolt as Dirty Harry Callahan, in the Dirty Harry series of movies. Almost overnight, Eastwood, the strong, silent hero signified what most of us wished we could be: self-assured, brave and fearless; a type of man who made up his own rules, lived by them and of course, won the battle for our side – the good guys!

However the men, whom the popular culture has held up as our icons over these many years, have views which almost coincide with those of our Deist Founding Fathers!! Webster's dictionary defines Deism "as a movement or system of thought advocating natural religion, emphasizing morality, and in the 18th century *denying the interference of the Creator with the laws of the universe or simply put – God created the earth and walked away"!*

John Wayne and Clint Eastwood did not outright deny the Creator Jesus Christ.

But when Wayne had an opportunity to state his beliefs, he said " *"I've always had a deep faith that there is a supreme being....there has to be....The fact that He's let me stick around a little longer, or She's let me stick around a little longer, certainly goes great with me!!!"*[33]

Clint Eastwood also had his chance to explain his beliefs to David Frost once on national TV and said this when asked by Frost "if God was important to him", Clint said" *'I'm just not a member of an organized religion. But I've always felt very strongly about things, I guess. Especially when I'm out in nature. I guess that's why I've done so many wide open films in nature. But religion is, I think, a very personal thing....*"[34]

---

[33] Ray Comfort, What Hollywood Believes (Genesis Publishing Group, 2004), p. 66.
[34] Patrick McGilligan, CLINT, the Life & Legend, (New York, NY: St. Martin's Press, 1999), p. 29.

Founding Fathers George Washington, Benjamin Franklin were both Deists as well. Thomas Jefferson is the best known Deist. Washington's beliefs were detailed in a book called "Washington and Religion" by Paul F. Boller. In this book, eyewitnesses to the great Washington said : "often said in my hearing, though very sorrowfully, of course, that while Washington was very deferential to religion and its ceremonies, like nearly all the founders of the Republic, he was not a Christian, but a Deist...!!"[35] (Pastor Arthur Bradford). 5

Jefferson is no better. He once considered himself to be a Unitarian as well as a deist. Here is what he said about the Bible and God's Truth in discussing the book or the Revelation "... (they are) merely the ravings of a maniac, no more worthy nor capable of explanation than the incoherencies of our own nightly dreams."[36]

He called the book of Revelation "manic ravings" that contained their "incoherencies". Webster's Dictionary defines a Unitarian as "one who believes in the oneness of God as opposed to traditional Christian belief in the Trinity or the Father, Son, and Holy Spirit."

These facts will surprise a lot of Christians and even preachers who keep contending that our Founding Fathers were the "biggest Christians and evangelists" in the world! But "facts are facts!" In fact it was Deism and Unitarianism which began this country's slide into 20th Century moral relativism.

EASTWOOD'S WORDS TO LIVE BY!

The big hero of the late 20th century - Clint Eastwood, a few years ago, released his own TEN RULES A MAN SHOULD

---

[35] "Washington and Religion", Paul Boller, Southern Methodist University Press, (1963) http://www.positiveatheism.org/hist/quotes/washington.htm.
[36] Charles B. Stanford, The Religious Life of Thomas Jefferson, (University of Virginia Press, 1987).

LIVE BY. Some of them can apply to the courage of The Continental Army crossing the Delaware! While they sound somewhat good, they are not scriptural. Please, judge for yourself. The Ten Rules were first published in Men's Journal, February 2004 edition. Here they are:

1. Call your own shots
2. Be fearless
3. Keep moving
4. Love your job
5. Speak softly
6. Don't be predictable
7. Find a good woman
8. Learn to play the piano
9. You are what you drive
10. Avoid extreme makeovers

Let us examine this to see how it squares with being a man or woman of God. God is not a self-described Libertarian like Eastwood who believes in absolute free will and unrestricted liberty of thought and action.

A child of God does not live on his or her own free will, but IN the Will of the One who saved us, because *"He who overcomes, I will make him a pillar in the temple of My God, and he will not go out from it anymore; and I will write on him the name of My God, and the name of the city of My God, the new Jerusalem, which comes down out of heaven from My God, and My new name"* (Jesus in Revelation 3:12).

A child of God does not run wild with the thoughts of this world, no matter how well intentioned, but has a mind of *"bringing every thought captive into captivity to the obedience of Christ'* (2 Cor. 10: 5b; NKJV).

A child of God does not go off doing our own thing because on Judgment Day *"each man's work will become evident; for the day will show it because it is to be revealed with*

fire, and the fire itself will test the quality of each man's work."
(1 Cor. 3:13).

EASTWOOD'S RULES, MODIFIED BY THE WORD OF GOD

1. Let God call the shots (Psalm 119:26)
2. Be Fearless because of Christ (2 Timothy 1:7)
3. Don't keep moving; *"Be still and know that I am God."(* Psalm 46:10)
4. Love the Lord Your God (Matthew 22:37) and NOT worldly things.
5. Season your speech: *"Let your speech always be with grace, as though seasoned with salt, so that you will know how you should respond to each person"* (Colossians 4:6).
6. Don't be predictable, be transparent *"But above all, my brethren, do not swear, either by heaven or by earth or with any other oath; but your yes is to be yes, and your no, no, so that you may not fall under judgment"* (James 5:12).
7. Men, pray the Lord to lead you to the wife He selected for you, before the Foundation of the World; women, vice versa, the same; *"He who finds a wife finds a good thing and obtains favor from the LORD"* (Proverbs 18:22).
8. Rejoice in the Music of the Lord: *"speaking to one another in psalms and hymns and spiritual songs, singing and making melody with your heart to the Lord"* (Ephesians 5:19).
9. If you are the driver, the wrong man's driving! Secondly, you are who you are in Christ. You are not who the world defines you (which is by what you do for a living) but you are *"those who have been sanctified in Christ Jesus, saints by calling, with all*

who in every place call on the name of our Lord Jesus Christ, their Lord and ours" (Ephesians 1:1).
10. Don't avoid "extreme makeovers"! *"Jesus answered, "Most assuredly, I say to you, unless one is born of water and the Spirit, he cannot enter the kingdom of God. That which is born of the flesh is flesh, and that which is born of the Spirit is spirit. Do not marvel that I said to you, 'You must be born again.' The wind blows where it wishes, and you hear the sound of it, but cannot tell where it comes from and where it goes. So is everyone who is born of the Spirit."* (John 3:5-8, NKJV).

One book I recommend to anyone who is interested in the beliefs of several of our great celebrities of the past and present is "What Hollywood believes" by one of my favorite people – Ray Comfort (Genesis Publishing, 2004). What you see in the book about people, whom you once thought were Christians would surprise you!

In the final analysis, it is obvious. A real man is a sold out, submissive, surrendered, smiling, Spirit-filled son of the Son of God. A real man is Christ's man. A real woman is all of that and the daughter of Christ. Together as a body of Christ we are now part of the Last Adam. When we return to the Garden of Eden in the New Heavens and Earth with Christ our Savior, King and Priest, we shall be once again be called man (Genesis 5:2).

Scripture says we will have a new name and live forever with Him. The Angel in Revelation 22 says *"the Kingdom of God is now with man"*....that is us my friends – but only if we are truly sons and daughters of Jesus Christ. There is no other way. There is no other religion and He is the Beginning and the End. He is the Lord of my life. He is all I need. He is my Sustainer, Redeemer, Counselor, Priest, King and Commander in Chief. I am ready to die for Him. How do I know all this? BECAUSE HE, WHO BEGAN A GOOD WORK IN ME, LIVES IN ME! AMEN

Bernie Lutchman

PRAY THE NAMES OF CHRIST

One of the most amazing acts of Worship is praying the Scriptures. What can be more honoring to God than you have His people, reverently and sincerely, read His Word back to Him! The following is a list of 177 names of Jesus Christ. Why does the world hate Him? Why do European and other Western secularists want to keep His name out of everything in every day life? Why are peaceful Gideons prosecuted in the Florida Keys for passing out Bibles on public sidewalks, in violation of the First Amendment? Why are Christians murdered and persecuted in India, Pakistan, China, Africa and other pagan cultures? Why? Because of the Name!

Read this list prayerfully. Look up the verses and you will know why the world hates us….because they first hated Him, and therefore His Name. Each verse below reveals something about the Nature of Christ.

For example 1 John 2:1 (NLT) says *"My dear children, I am writing this to you so that you will not sin. But if anyone does sin, we have an Advocate who pleads our case before the Father. He is Jesus Christ, the One who is truly righteous"*.

The word "ADVOCATE" comes out of two Latin words "ad" and "vocare", meaning to summon or call for counsel. When we sin or fall short of the Glory of God, our High Priest Jesus stands before the Father and says "forgive him/her…that one's Mine". In effect the Father then remembers our sin no more….and it is placed far from Him as far as the east is from the west. If we keep doing the same sin over and over though, we have a HUGE problem and apart from grieving Christ's Holy Spirit, we are then subject to intense discipline from God.

The prayer here would be to thank the Lord Jesus for the VERY fact that He intercedes for us before the Father. If anyone reading this has ever been in a legal situation or a hearing at work etc, or even in a cause where you need a professional to speak for you, it is well known how important an Advocate is.

Christ is more than just interceding for us before the Throne, He is our Mediator. This fact alone should be more than enough to trigger our gratitude. So we pray Thanksgiving into this verse. This is how we pray the Names of Christ. One day in Heaven, it will be perfectly clear, why this is such a powerful devotion!

177 Names of Christ and Verses[37]

1.	Abraham's Seed	Genesis 22:18; Galatians 3:16
2.	Advocate	1 John 2:1
3.	Almighty	Revelation 1:8
4.	Alpha and Omega	Revelation 1:8; 22:13
5.	Amen	Revelation 3:14
6.	Angel	Genesis 48:16; Exodus 23:20-21
7.	Angel of God's Presence	Isaiah 63:9
8.	Angel of the Lord	Exodus 3:2; Judges 13:15-22
9.	Apostle	Hebrews 3:1
10.	Arm of the Lord	Isaiah 51:9; 53:1
11.	Author and Finisher of our faith	Hebrews 12:2
12.	Author of eternal salvation	Hebrews 5:9
13.	Beginning of the creation of God	Revelation 3:14
14.	Beloved	Ephesians 1:6

---

[37]http://www.promiselandchrysalis.com/templates/System/details.asp?id=30821&PID=242607.

15.	Beloved Son	Matthew 12:18
16.	Blessed and only Potentate	1 Timothy 6:15
17.	Branch	Jeremiah 23:5; Zechariah 3:8; 6:12
18.	Bread of Life	John 6:35, 48
19.	Bridegroom	Matthew 9:15
20.	Bright and Morning Star	Revelation 22:16
21.	Captain of Salvation	Hebrews 2:10
22.	Captain of the Lord's Host	Joshua 5:14-15
23.	Carpenter	Mark 6:3
24.	Carpenter's Son	Matthew 13:55
25.	Chief Cornerstone	Ephesians 2:20; 1 Peter 2:6
26.	Chief Shepherd	1 Peter 5:4
27.	Christ	Matthew 16:20; Mark 14:16; Luke 23:2
28.	Christ Jesus	Acts 19:4; Romans 3:24; 8:1; 1 Corinthians 1:2, 30
29.	Christ Jesus our Lord	Romans 8:39; 1 Timothy 1:12
30.	Christ of God	Luke 9:20
31.	Christ the Lord	Luke 2:11
32.	Commander	Isaiah 55:4
33.	Consolation of Israel	Luke 2:25
34.	Cornerstone	Matthew 21:42; Ephesians 2:20
35.	Counselor	Isaiah 9:6
36.	Creator	John 1:3
37.	David	Jeremiah 30:9; Ezekiel 34:23
38.	Dayspring	Luke 1:78
39.	Deliverer	Romans 11:26
40.	Desire of all nations	Haggai 2:7
41.	Door	John 10:7

42.	Elect of God	Isaiah 42:1
43.	Eternal life	1 John 1:2; 5:20
44.	Everlasting Father	Isaiah 9:6
45.	Faithful and True	Revelation 19:11
46.	Faithful Witness	Revelation 1:5; 3:14
47.	First and Last	Revelation 1:17; 2:8
48.	Firstborn	Psalm 89:27; Hebrews 1:6; Revelation 1:5
49.	Forerunner	Hebrews 6:20
50.	Fountain	Zechariah 13:1
51.	Glory of the Lord	Isaiah 40:5
52.	God	Isaiah 40:9; John 20:28
53.	God blessed forever	Romans 9:5
54.	God's fellow	Zechariah 13:7
55.	Good Shepherd	John 10:14
56.	Governor	Matthew 2:6
57.	Great High Priest	Hebrews 4:14
58.	Head of the Church	Ephesians 5:23; Colossians 1:18
59.	Heir of all things	Hebrews 1:2
60.	High Priest	Hebrews 4:14
61.	Holy Child	Acts 4:27
62.	Holy One	Psalm 16:10; Acts 2:27; 3:14
63.	Holy One of God	Mark 1:24
64.	Holy One of Israel	Isaiah 41:14; 54:5
65.	Horn of salvation	Luke 1:69
66.	I AM	Exodus 3:14; John 8:58
67.	Image of God	2 Corinthians 4:4
68.	Immanuel	Isaiah 7:14; Matthew 1:23
69.	Jesus	Matthew 1:21; 1 Thessalonians 1:10

70.	Jesus Christ	Matthew 1:1
71.	Jesus of Nazareth	Matthew 21:11; Mark 1:24; Luke 24:19
72.	Judge	Acts 10:42; 2 Timothy 4:8
73.	Judge of Israel	Micah 5:1
74.	Just One	Acts 7:52; 22:14
75.	King	Zechariah 9:9; Matthew 21:5
76.	King of Glory	Psalms 24:7-10
77.	King of Israel	John 1:49
78.	King of Kings	1 Timothy 6:15; Revelation 17:14
79.	King of peace	Hebrews 7:2
80.	King of righteousness	Hebrews 7:2
81.	King of saints	Revelation 15:3
82.	King of Salem	Hebrews 7:1
83.	King of the Jews	Matthew 2:2; 27:37; John 19:19
84.	King of Zion	Matthew 21:25
85.	Lamb	Revelation 5:6,12; 13:8; 21:22; 22:3
86.	Lamb of God	John 1:29,36
87.	Lawgiver	Isaiah 33:22
88.	Leader	Isaiah 55:4
89.	Life	John 14:6; Colossians 3:4; 1 John 1:2
90.	Light of the world	John 1:8; 8:12
91.	Lily of the valleys	Song of Solomon 2:1
92.	Lion of the tribe of Judah	Revelation 5:5
93.	Living bread	John 6:51
94.	Living stone	1 Peter 2:4
95.	Lord and Savior	2 Peter 1:11; 3:18
96.	Lord Christ	Colossians 3:24
97.	Lord God Almighty	Revelation 15:3

DANGER ZONE

98.	Lord God of the holy prophets	Revelation 22:6
99.	Lord Jesus	Acts 7:59; Colossians 3:17
100.	Lord Jesus Christ	Acts 11:17; 16:31; 20:21
101.	Lord of all	Acts 10:36
102.	Lord of glory	1 Corinthians 2:8; James 2:1
103.	Lord of Hosts	Isaiah 44:6
104.	Lord of Lords	1 Timothy 6:15; Revelation 17:14; 19:16
105.	Lord our righteousness	Jeremiah 23:6; 33:16
106.	Man of sorrows	Isaiah 53:3
107.	Mediator	1 Timothy 2:5
108.	Messenger of the covenant	Malachi 3:1
109.	Messiah	Daniel 9:25; John 1:41
110.	Mighty God	Isaiah 9:6
111.	Mighty One of Israel	Isaiah 30:29
112.	Mighty One of Jacob	Isaiah 49:26; 60:16
113.	Morningstar	Revelation 22:16; 2 Peter 1:19
114.	Most Holy	Daniel 9:24
115.	Nazarene	Matthew 9:23
116.	Offspring of David	Revelation 22:16
117.	Only begotten	John 1:14
118.	Only begotten Son	John 1:18
119.	Our Passover	1 Corinthians 5:7
120.	Potentate	1 Timothy 6:15
121.	Power of God	1 Corinthians 1:24
122.	Prince	Acts 5:31
123.	Prince of life	Acts 3:15
124.	Prince of peace	Isaiah 9:6
125.	Prince of the kings of the earth	Revelation 1:5
126.	Prophet	Matthew 21:11; Luke

		24:19; John 7:40
127.	Rabbi	John 1:49
128.	Rabboni	John 20:16
129.	Ransom	1 Timothy 2:6
130.	Redeemer	Job 19:25; Isaiah 59:20; 60:16
131.	Resurrection and life	John 11:25
132.	Rock	1 Corinthians 10:4
133.	Rock of offence	1 Peter 2:8
134.	Root of David	Revelation 5:5; 22:16
135.	Root of Jesse	Isaiah 11:10
136.	Rose of Sharon	Song of Solomon 2:1
137.	Ruler of Israel	Micah 5:2
138.	Savior	Luke 2:11; 2 Peter 2:20; 3:18
139.	Savior of the body	Ephesians 5:23
140.	Scepter	Numbers 24:17
141.	Second Adam	1 Corinthians 15:45
142.	Second Man	1 Corinthians 15:47
143.	Seed of David	2 Timothy 2:8
144.	Seed of woman	Genesis 3:15
145.	Servant	Isaiah 42:1; 52:13; 53:11; Acts 4:30
146.	Servant of Rulers	Isaiah 49:7
147.	Shepherd	Mark 14:27
148.	Shepherd and overseer of souls	1 Peter 2:25
149.	Shepherd of Israel	Psalm 80:1
150.	Shiloh	Genesis 49:10
151.	Son of David	Matthew 9:27
152.	Son of God	Luke 1:35; John 1:49
153.	Son of Joseph	John 6:42
154.	Son of man	John 5:27
155.	Son of the Blessed	Mark 14:61
156.	Son of the Father	2 John 1:3
157.	Son of the Highest	Luke 1:32

158.	Star	Numbers 24:17
159.	Stone of stumbling	1 Peter 2:8
160.	Sun of righteousness	Malachi 4:2
161.	Sure foundation	Isaiah 28:16
162.	Surety	Hebrews 7:22
163.	Teacher	Matthew 23:8; John 3:2
164.	Tender plant	Isaiah 53:2
165.	True God	1 John 5:20
166.	True light	John 1:9
167.	True vine	John 15:1
168.	Truth	John 14:6
169.	Vine	John 15:1
170.	Way	John 14:6
171.	Wisdom	Proverbs 8:12
172.	Wisdom of God	1 Corinthians 1:24
173.	Witness	Isaiah 55:4; Revelation 1:5
174.	Wonderful	Isaiah 9:6
175.	Word	John 1:1; 1 John 5:7
176.	Word of God	Revelation 19:13
177.	Word of life	1 John 1:1

REVELATION!

WDJW (what did Jesus write?)

John 8: 3-11 NLT reads: *"As He was speaking, the teachers of religious law and the Pharisees brought a woman who had been caught in the act of adultery. They put her in front of the crowd.* ⁴ *"Teacher," they said to Jesus, "this woman was caught in the act of adultery.* ⁵ *The Law of Moses says to stone her. What do you say?"*

*⁶ They were trying to trap him into saying something they could use against him, but **Jesus stooped down and wrote in the dust with his finger**. ⁷ They kept demanding an answer, so He stood up again and said, "All right, but let the one who has never sinned throw the first stone!" ⁸**Then He stooped down again and wrote in the dust**. ⁹ When the accusers heard this, they slipped away one by one, beginning with the oldest, until only Jesus was left in the middle of the crowd with the woman. ¹⁰ Then Jesus stood up again and said to the woman, "Where are your accusers? Didn't even one of them condemn you?" ¹¹ "No, Lord," she said. And Jesus said, "Neither do I. Go and sin no more."*

Look at the two bold underlined sentences again. Both times Jesus wrote on the ground with His Fingers. When the pastor of Springfield Bible Church, John Standard was preaching out of John 8 on this passage, and came up to this, the Spirit of the Lord gave me a revelation which still floors me.

No one, no theologian or writer or preacher can prove what Jesus wrote on the ground. Neither can I. All I am saying is what the Lord directed me to on this Sunday morning during the message, and I believe it.

Look at Daniel 5:25-28 "²⁵ "And this is the inscription that was written: MENE, MENE, TEKEL, UPHARSIN. ²⁶ This *is* the interpretation of *each* word. MENE: God has numbered your kingdom, and finished it; ²⁷ **TEKEL: You have been weighed in the balances, and found wanting;** ²⁸ PERES: Your kingdom has been divided, and given to the Medes and Persians." (Emphasis mine)

It is my contention, from listening to the Lord and His directing me immediately to this Scripture, that Jesus wrote **TEKEL** in the dirt that day!

In John 8:16, John specifically says *"Jesus bent down and* **started to write on the ground with His Finger***"*. The last time we saw the handwriting with a Finger is Daniel 5:5 *"Suddenly* **the fingers of a human hand appeared and wrote** *on the plaster of* *the wall, near the lamp stand in the royal palace. The king watched the hand as it wrote".*

Is this out of the realm of His possibility? NO!!! A thousand times NO!!!

During a fast a few years ago, He revealed, (and I stand on this), to me that He wrote the 10 Commandments on Mt. Sinai on the tablet. He is called the Word of God and in the Beginning was the Word. He is the Creator of all things. I know He wrote the Tablets. He was in the Pillar of Fire. He was the Rock that Moses struck in anger. In fact Moses had to die before they got to the Promised Land because of this disobedient sin! 1 Corinthians 10:4 says the Rock He struck was Christ. So Christ was everywhere on earth in Spirit before His humble Birth in Bethlehem.

Sure John 8:16 may be the first time the God/Man Jesus was seen physically to write something on earth, but His was the hand in Belshazzar's palace on that day!

Why do I say He wrote "**TEKEL**"? This means "you have been weighed in the scales and found DEFICIENT"!! Now, before I got saved, I was TEKEL...and not tickled! In fact the world is too pickled in its own corruption to see what the Son of Man is saying to them. Conversely Daniel was told by the Angel of God, he is *"highly esteemed"* in Daniel 9:23 – the opposite of TEKEL!

Therefore when Jesus wrote **TEKEL** on the ground, He had the same message for the Pharisees….namely "men…teachers of the Law and Pharisees, you hypocrites….who are you to attempt to stone this woman….I have weighed <u>YOU</u> in the scales and you have no moral authority to do this! You are more in desperate need of a Savior as she is, now back off"!!

Am I nuts? I don't think so! I just love Jesus! In my humble opinion, this answers the question: "WHAT DID JESUS WRITE, or WDJW"?

Two things here – God is God and we are not. Also, He can speak to whom He pleases!

This is not the place for a discussion on the subject of *"God still speaks today"*. On the surface, this question is ludicrous! Of course He does! Because so many have abused their fellow man by claiming *"God told me to do ...."* doubt and ridicule face those who make such a claim. This is completely understandable and we all condemn this garbage. Many a heresy, hurt and hateful act have been committed by people who claimed they had "clear instructions" from God.

So, how does a man or woman of God discern if the voice in their heads or in the very innermost part of the soul belongs to the Almighty in Heaven?

HOW TO DISCERN THE VOICE OF GOD

We all remember the story of the little boy Samuel from 1 Samuel Chapter 1, when the Lord God Himself called Samuel's name four times – trying to get his attention.

1 Samuel 1:10 (NIV) says:"The LORD came and stood there, calling as at the other times, "Samuel! Samuel!" Then Samuel said, "Speak, for your servant is listening."

Note something here – the LORD STOOD THERE!! STOOD! In His powerful omnipresence, the LORD was physically placing His Call on the future prophet's wife – personally! There are countless other accounts in the Bible and in the 2000 years since the Cross of the Lord intervening in the lives and affairs of men.

More times than not, God ONLY reveals Himself to those whom He has already saved. The three most glaring exceptions are the Burning Bush and Moses; 1 Samuel 1:7; the Apostle Paul on the Road to Damascus and my personal favorite – the Prophet Daniel!!

Here is what the Word says about Daniel in Chapter 10:11 (NASB) *"He said to me, "O Daniel, man of high esteem, understand the words that I am about to tell you and stand upright, for I have now been sent to you." And when he had spoken this word to me, I stood up trembling".*

How many of us, no matter what our station in life, would love to hear DIRECTLY from Heaven that "we are men (and women) of HIGH ESTEEM"?!! The word "esteem" means here the following – God looked down from Heaven approvingly, and just loved and held His son Daniel in such high regard, He sent one of His chief messengers to tell this to the prophet!

But how can WE, as mere mortals operating in the 21st century of secular humanism, become this way? Is God's favor only for His chosen spokesmen in the Bible? Did He only speak to those men and women like Deborah, Daniel and John the Revelator and then leave us on our own? No! A thousand times NO!

Daniel 10:12 (NASB) continues *"Then he said to me, "Do not be afraid, Daniel, for from the first day that you set your heart on understanding this and on humbling yourself before your God, your words were heard, and I have come in response to your words"*

Reexamine Daniel's conduct in the Danger Zone of the pagan King's palace:

- He refused to eat the king's meat, which was not only sacrificed to some worthless god, but was not prepared according to God's health laws from the Torah.
- He, Shadrach, Meshach and Abednego ate only veggies in what we now call the "Daniel Fast" for a week. After that week, they looked healthier than anyone who had eaten the king's meat and drank from his wine.
- He prayed. He fasted. He obeyed.
- Look at what God's Messenger said to Daniel in verse 12 – Daniel set his "Heart on understanding"(more on this word below).
- He humbled himself before God.

Therefore, in light of all of the above – God listened. When God listens, He speaks in return and gives revelation to His people. My goal is to walk with Christ is such a manner.

By the way, God will never lead you away from His closed and written Word, found in all 66 Books of the Bible. If you think you hear "a word from the LORD" and a spirit tells you to go look in the Koran or some psychology book for an answer – you are NOT hearing from the ONE TRUE GOD!

The LORD Himself said in Joel 2:28 (NASB) *"It will come about after this That I will pour out My Spirit on all mankind; And your sons and daughters will prophesy, Your old men will dream dreams, Your young men will see visions"*

This is also true. I have had several dreams and visions, which have confirmed personal matters for me, as well as visions of things to come. Dreams have come early in the morning, most times, which reveal either deliverance from an issue or confirmation of a direction or a prophetic vision. This type of intervention by the Lord is spoken of specifically in Psalm 127:2 He gives to His beloved even in his sleep.

There was another time when I was taken up, quickly (again…this first happened in 1988 on another encounter) into the heavens and shown many white statues, only to look down to see a personnel carrier, ready for take-off, with no engine or motor (for the Lord is its engine) and many of the remnant sitting in it. My friends, who are praying pastors, interpreted this dream for me the same way, unbeknownst to each other.

Man cannot come up with these things on his own. It is God and God alone who gives these amazing blessings to His people. He chooses whom He wishes to visit this way. Many in the Christian world have said God has stopped speaking to and visiting His people when the Bible was closed in Revelation 22.

This would render Joel 2:28 untrue! Also, I would not believe the charlatans and showmen who claim a special word from the Lord "that you too can have if you send me $1600 to sow a seed…and all your bills will be paid and you will have a new Cadillac"!!!! Do NOT buy that for one minute. These are false gospels from the pit, the very pit of hell. These Elmer Gantry types will be held accountable one day for this, so let not your heart be troubled.

At the same time, do NOT despise either the Discipline or the Dispensation of His Grace and Riches to even the lowliest person in the church. In essence – never try to fit the Lord your God into your tiny neat little box, when He is Infinite and all powerful and can do just about anything He pleases.

Finally, early in this section on HOW to discern the voice of God (the Holy Spirit will reveal Him as True), I mentioned Daniel 10:12 NASB: *"Then he said to me, "Do not be afraid, Daniel, for from the first day that you set your heart on understanding this and on humbling yourself before your God, your words were heard, and I have come in response to your words"*

The Messenger from God (who is not named, but who we believe was either Gabriel or Michael) said *".....you set your heart on understanding this and humbling yourself..."*

The original Biblical word for "understanding" is "BIN" (pronounced "bean"). This means to consider completely; becoming completely aware of; to examine carefully or seek full knowledge of …and more! Daniel relentlessly and faithfully sought that knowledge.

When he came to the full realization of GOD (as much as the puny human mind can comprehend) and just WHO the LORD is, the next part of the verse said Daniel humbled himself!

This is what happens when we realize and see the God Whom Job encountered in Job chapters 38-42 and was left without a word (after mouthing off about God for a large portion of the Book of Job).

My contention is once we become like Daniel in Godly wisdom/knowledge, which leads to humility/surrender to Christ, then He will not only reveal more of Himself and the Work of the Kingdom now and to come, but will show you great and marvelous things to come.

At this point, you will know Who is speaking and discern that HE – the Holy Spirit – is the Spirit of the Incomparable Christ. He is the Christ and Lord and Savior who has taken us away from the Danger Zone, into a realm of Peace, joy, happiness and contentment where the Father lives. Amen.

THE INCOMPARABLE CHRIST

Colossians 1: 15-20 (NLT) lovingly explains our Lord:

- [15] Christ is the visible image of the invisible God. He existed before anything was created and is supreme over all creation,
[16] for through him God created everything in the

heavenly realms and on earth. He made the things we can see and the things we can't see—such as thrones, kingdoms, rulers, and authorities in the unseen world. Everything was created through him and for him. [17] He existed before anything else, and he holds all creation together. [18] Christ is also the head of the church, which is his body. He is the beginning, supreme over all who rise from the dead. So he is first in everything. [19] For God in all his fullness was pleased to live in Christ, [20] and through him God reconciled everything to himself. He made peace with everything in heaven and on earth by means of Christ's blood on the cross.

There is just NO ONE, EVER, who can ever compare to the Lord Jesus Christ. He is not just a prophet or a deity or some made up thing which the pagan religions of the world made up. He is Jesus (He who will save the people from their sins) and the Christ, the Anointed One, the Messiah!

About the Author

Bernie Lutchman is disciple of the Lord Jesus Christ, evangelist, prayer leader and author. He has been a leader of Men's Ministry in Springfield, Illinois since 1996, is the Vice President of Business Men In Christ, an established and growing volunteer men's service and evangelistic ministry in Central Illinois. Bernie has also been the official leader of Springfield's National Day of Prayer Annual observance at the Illinois State Capitol since 2006. He is involved in several prayer and outreach ministries, including monthly Ministry Outreach to several area-wide Seniors Nursing and Assisted Living homes in the Springfield Metro area, with his family. Bernie also teaches on the Bible on a weekly Community Access Channel for Comcast Cable in the Sangamon County area since 2008.

Bernie Lutchman has a B.A. from Acadia University in Nova Scotia. He is certified by the American Association of Christian Counselors, and has a Diploma from the Institute of Bible Studies of Liberty University. Bernie is married to Vicki. They have three children Bernie III, Sam and Sarah. They live in Chatham, Illinois.

www.ingramcontent.com/pod-product-compliance
Lightning Source LLC
Chambersburg PA
CBHW061440040426
42450CB00007B/1138